THE WAY
PEOPLE
LIVE

Life Among the Pirates

Titles in The Way People Live series include:

Life Among the Pirates

Among the

by Stuart A. Kallen

Lucent Books, P.O. Box 289011, San Diego, CA 92198-9011

Library of Congress Cataloging-in-Publication Data

Kallen, Stuart A., 1955–
    Life among the pirates / by Stuart A. Kallen.
        p.   cm. — (The way people live)
    Includes bibliographical references and index.
    Summary: Discusses facts and myths about pirates who sailed and
plundered on the seas from the sixteenth to the nineteenth century.
        ISBN 1-56006-393-9 (alk. paper)
    1. Pirates—Juvenile literature.   [1. Pirates.]   I. Title.   II. Series.
G535.K14   1999
910.4'5—dc21   98-15468
                                                                              CIP
                                                                              AC

Copyright 1999 by Lucent Books, Inc., P.O. Box 289011, San Diego, California
92198-9011

Printed in the U.S.A.

Contents

Discovering the Humanity in Us All

The Way People Live series focuses on pockets of human culture. Some of these are current cultures, like the Eskimos of the Arctic; others no longer exist, such as the Jewish ghetto in Warsaw during World War II. What many of these cultural pockets share, however, is the fact that they have been viewed before, but not completely understood.

To really understand any culture, it is necessary to strip the mind of the common notions we hold about groups of people. These stereotypes are the archenemies of learning. It does not even matter whether the stereotypes are positive or negative; they are confining and tight. Removing them is a challenge that's not easily met, as anyone who has ever tried it will admit. Ideas that do not fit into the templates we create are unwelcome visitors—ones we would prefer remain quietly in a corner or forgotten room.

The cowboy of the Old West is a good example of such confining roles. The cowboy was courageous, yet soft-spoken. His time (it is always a he, in our template) was spent alternatively saving a rancher's daughter from certain death on a runaway stagecoach, or shooting it out with rustlers. At times, of course, he was likely to get a little crazy in town after a trail drive, but for the most part, he was the epitome of inner strength. It is disconcerting to find out that the cowboy is human, even a bit childish. Can it really be true that cowboys would line up to help the cook on the trail drive grind coffee, just hoping he would give them a little stick of peppermint candy that came with the coffee shipment? The idea of tough cowboys vying with one another to help "Coosie" (as they called their cooks) for a bit of candy seems silly and out of place.

So is the vision of Eskimos playing video games and watching MTV, living in prefab housing in the Arctic. It just does not fit with what "Eskimo" means. We are far more comfortable with snow igloos and whale blubber, harpoons and kayaks.

Although the cultures dealt with in Lucent's The Way People Live series are often historically and socially well known, the emphasis is on the personal aspects of life. Groups of people, while unquestionably affected by their politics and their governmental structures, are more than those institutions. How do people in a particular time and place educate their children? What do they eat? And how do they build their houses? What kinds of work do they do? What kinds of games do they enjoy? The answers to these questions bring these cultures to life. People's lives are revealed in the particulars and only by knowing the particulars can we understand these cultures' will to survive and their moments of weakness and greatness.

This is not to say that understanding politics does not help to understand a culture. There is no question that the Warsaw ghetto, for example, was a culture that was brought about by the politics and social ideas of Adolf Hitler and the Third Reich. But the Jews who were crowded together in the ghetto cannot be understood by the Reich's politics. Their life was a day-to-day battle for existence, and the creativity and methods they used to prolong their lives is a vital story of human perseverance that would be denied by focusing only on the institutions of Hitler's Germany. Knowing that children as young as five or six outwitted Nazi guards on a daily basis, that Jewish policemen helped the Germans control the ghetto, that children attended secret schools in the ghetto and even earned diplomas—these are the things that reveal the fabric of life, that can inspire, intrigue, and amaze.

Books in The Way People Live series allow both the casual reader and the student to see humans as victims, heroes, and onlookers. And although humans act in ways that can fill us with feelings of sorrow and revulsion, it is important to remember that "hero," "predator," and "victim" are dangerous terms. Heaping undue pity or praise on people reduces them to objects, and strips them of their humanity.

Seeing the Jews of Warsaw only as victims is to deny their humanity. Seeing them only as they appear in surviving photos, staring at the camera with infinite sadness, is limiting, both to them and to those who want to understand them. To an object of pity, the only appropriate response becomes "Those poor creatures!" and that reduces both the quality of their struggle and the depth of their despair. No one is served by such two-dimensional views of people and their cultures.

With this in mind, The Way People Live series strives to flesh out the traditional, two-dimensional views of people in various cultures and historical circumstances. Using a wide variety of primary quotations—the words not only of the politicians and government leaders, but of the real people whose lives are being examined—each book in the series attempts to show an honest and complete picture of a culture removed from our own by time or space.

By examining cultures in this way, the reader will notice not only the glaring differences from his or her own culture, but also will be struck by the similarities. For indeed, people share common needs—warmth, good company, stability, and affirmation from others. Ultimately, seeing how people really live, or have lived can only enrich our understanding of ourselves.

The Famous Age of Pirates

It is a story as old as civilization itself: A ship is sailing across the sea when it is suddenly attacked. Desperate, armed men clamor aboard, knock down the captain, and make off with the ship's cargo. That is the definition of piracy. Piracy is the act of plundering on the high seas. It has been happening on a daily basis for more than eight thousand years. And it still happens today.

The art of piracy goes back to the world's first great civilizations. Pirates are simply common—and not so common—criminals who break society's rules. Twenty-five hundred years ago, pirates plowed the Aegean Sea, stealing tin, silver, copper, and grain from Greek merchants. Later, in Roman times, pirates in swift galleys stole wine and olive oil from vessels on the Mediterranean. Around A.D. 800, vikings from Scandinavia roamed the oceans, sacking, pillaging, and plundering from the Baltic to France to Turkey.

The Golden Age of Piracy

The era associated with swashbuckling buccaneers, however, began around 1520. At that time Spanish galleons loaded with Aztec gold, silver, and jewels became targets in the Caribbean Sea. For the next two centuries, the players changed, but the stage remained the same. The Caribbean was host to pirates from almost every country in the world.

By 1691, piracy was out of control in and around the Caribbean waters. Thousands of pirates plundered and looted at will. Entire islands were controlled by pirates, and the economies of great European nations hung in the balance. That era, which ended around 1723, was called the golden age of piracy. And it was a golden age—for the pirates.

While pirate Charles Bellamy was plundering a merchant ship off the coast of South Carolina in 1717, he told his victims: "I am a free prince and I have as much authority to make war on the whole World as he who has a hundred sail of ships at sea and an army of 100,000 men in the field."[1]

Drunken pirates revel in the port city of Charleston, South Carolina.

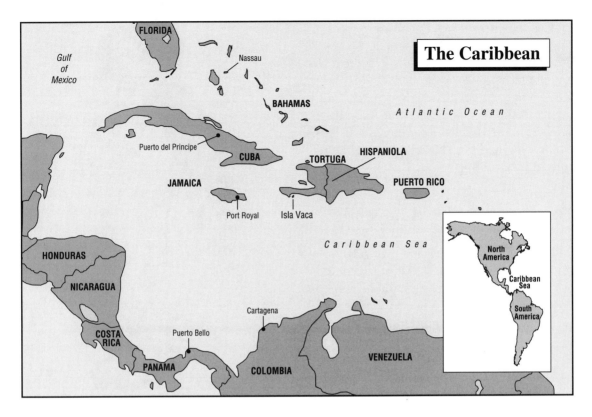

The Caribbean

Bellamy's claims may sound exaggerated today. But during piracy's golden age, thousands of desperadoes like Bellamy did rule the sea lanes of the world. They were young, drunk, uneducated, desperate, and armed to the teeth. So large was their treasure and so dastardly their deeds that some became legends in their own lifetimes.

Swashbuckling Desperadoes

Popular myth has portrayed pirates as daring, romantic rascals: captains dressed in gentlemanly finery, offset by the terror of a cutlass in the hand that had not been replaced by a metal hook; fearless crews wearing eye patches awaiting any opportunity to nab ships on the high seas.

Over the years pirates have become romantic legends. Countless books, plays, and movies have been written about swashbuckling desperadoes that plunder at sea. Like many other legends, these images combine fact with a healthy dose of fiction. The enduring portrait of pirates does not always square with reality.

Surprisingly, a number of pirate images are accurate. During the great age of piracy, from the 1500s to the early 1700s, pirates did wear cutlasses around their waists and pistols strapped to their chests. Some wore velvet clothes, silk scarves, and jewelry looted from merchant ships. And after having their limbs shot or cut off in battle, a few pirates did have hooks for hands and wooden poles for legs.

Many of the factual details of pirate life, however, have eluded the popular myth that has been handed down through three hundred years worth of ballads, poems, novels, magazine stories, comic strips, plays, and movies. The resulting image of pirates is tinged with a romantic element that was never given to pirates when they were alive and plundering the seven seas. Pirate attacks were often violent and ugly. Pirates inhumanly tortured, raped, and murdered thousands of their victims. Economic hardships, bankruptcy, and even starvation were the results of their looting.

Treasure Island and Beyond

So how did these vicious men ever get such a romantic image? As the threat of real pirates evaporated in the early 1800s, public perception of pirates began to change. Pirates were no longer regarded as murderers and thieves but as wild and free outlaws who played by their own rules. They robbed from the rich and laughed at authorities.

Fictional books and magazine stories about pirates blossomed during the nineteenth century. Many of these works became best-sellers. It seemed the pirate-hungry public could not get enough stories of the swashbuckling seamen.

Many of the images of pirates that remain today can be traced to Robert Louis Stevenson's 1883 story *Treasure Island*. The fictional Long John Silver of Stevenson's book is perhaps the best-known pirate in history. His left leg was cut off when he was hit by a cannonball. He did not have a wooden leg but was a "great, glowing, massive-shouldered fellow with a big red beard and a crutch; jovial, astoundingly clever, and with a laugh that rolled out like music."[2]

The first fifteen chapters of the tale were published—one per week—in a magazine called *Young Folks*. When the story was later published as a book, it proved to be very popular with adolescents and adults alike. The

A swashbuckling pirate brandishes a pistol and a cutlass, weapons commonly used by sea rogues.

story was adapted for the stage, and there have been at least five movies based on the novel.

Although *Treasure Island* was a work of fiction, Stevenson blended many facts about pirate life into the story, including tropical islands, schooners, parrots, one-legged seamen, and the phrase "yo-ho-ho and a bottle of rum."

The Hard Reality and the Payoff

While it is true that many pirates lived on tropical islands and kept parrots for pets, the hard reality of pirate life is not the stuff of storybooks. Death and misery stalked the pirate in dozens of ways. Life was spent under the burning tropical sun during the day and on the damp, chilly sea at night, and the threat of storms, gales, and hurricanes was constant. Diseases like scurvy, yellow fever, and dysentery shot through pirate crews, killing a great percentage. Thirst and starvation were as common as the rats and cockroaches that infested pirate ships. Pirates who were caught by the authorities were hanged. Sometimes their bodies were covered in tar and suspended in chains as a warning to others.

But looting a treasure ship was a pirate's reward. Suddenly, his clothes went from filthy rags to silk and velvet. Shipboard stale water and weak beer were replaced by French brandy and Italian wine. His rotting old scow was left behind as he took over a European-built, three-masted brigantine ship.

Most pirates, however, did not acquire such legendary booty. They were happy to steal the most mundane things. The average pirate stole little fishing boats, ropes and sails, sewing kits, tools, tobacco, and other necessities for daily life. Those who obtained vast wealth were a minority. Nine out of ten pirates never got rich, and the ones who did usually drank and gambled their money away within weeks.

Over the centuries, however, pirate reality has given way to pirate fiction. People trapped in mundane jobs and less-than-exciting lives have kept the pirate myth alive. To be free, to sail off on uncharted seas, to discover untold wealth—it is a dream as old as humankind itself.

The Great Age of Piracy

The 1500s were a time of heroes and explorers who chased their dreams across the seven seas. European sailors from Spain, Portugal, Italy, England, and France sailed across the globe in uncharted waters. Back home the words and deeds of these sailors were the subject of books, poems, songs, and plays. It was a dangerous life and the hardships were many. Death and disease stalked the sailors over every horizon.

European explorers did not set out to become heroes, however. They were searching for riches. In 1492 Christopher Columbus was the first European to set foot in the Americas, on the island he called San Salvador. One of the first questions he asked the Arawak people who lived there was "Where is the gold?" Columbus's view was shared by many explorers when he wrote, "Gold constitutes treasure and he who possesses it has all he needs in the world."[3]

Columbus never found the gold and riches he desired. But his voyages took him to the islands of Cuba, Puerto Rico, San Salvador, Jamaica, and Hispaniola (now Haiti). (Columbus mistakenly thought he was land-

Christopher Columbus plants the Spanish flag on the shores of the New World. Columbus traveled throughout the Caribbean in search of gold and treasure.

ing in the country of India. Because of Columbus's error, the islands are also known as the West Indies, and the natives who lived there as Indians.) Within fifty years of Columbus's voyage, the West Indies—and the Caribbean Sea between them—would become a haven for explorers and pirates alike. It was the stage on which the great age of piracy was played out from 1519 to the 1700s.

Plundering the Aztecs

The great age of piracy dawned one day in 1519. On the morning of April 21, six hundred Spanish soldiers landed on the eastern coast of Mexico near the modern-day city of Veracruz. The soldiers were led by Hernán Cortés and were armed with swords, muskets, pikes, cannons, and crossbows. The Aztec people were living in Mexico when the Spaniards invaded. The native Aztecs had not learned to use the wheel in their daily lives. They had never seen horses, guns, or cannons. But the Aztecs had a highly advanced civilization. Their capital city of Tenochtitlán was filled with awe-inspiring art, sculpture, and architecture. And it was all shimmering with gold, silver, and precious jewels.

When the Spanish soldiers reached Tenochtitlán, they were astounded by the wealth they found. Bernal Díaz del Castillo, a writer brought by Cortés to record the invasion, described it: "With such wonderful sights to gaze on, we did not know what to say, or if what we saw before our eyes was real."[4]

By 1521 Cortés had reduced Tenochtitlán to rubble. An estimated one hundred thousand natives were killed in bloody battles. Where the jewel of Aztec civilization once stood, Cortés began to build what is today Mexico City, while the Spanish systematically looted the Aztec Empire. By 1525 hundreds of

Hernán Cortés (center) and his soldiers slay the residents of Tenochtitlán, the seat of Aztec culture and wealth.

ships, called galleons, were returning to Spain overloaded with plundered Aztec treasure.

Stealing Inca Treasures

When the Spaniards saw the wealth possessed by the Aztecs, they began a relentless search for more. Rumors began to reach Spanish explorers of another rich empire ruled by the Inca people in the modern-day country of Peru in South America.

The land ruled by the Incas stretched more than two thousand miles across the peaks and valleys of the Andes Mountains. Like the Aztecs, the Incas had no guns or wheels. But, also like the Aztecs, Incan artists made fantastic ornaments of silver, gold, and jewels to honor their gods.

On November 15, 1532, a tiny force of 180 men, led by Francisco Pizarro, set out to conquer the Incas. Pizarro kidnapped the Inca leader, Atahuallpa, and demanded a roomful of gold jewelry as ransom. When it was delivered, the ornaments were melted down into bars of gold and distributed to the Spanish soldiers. One-fifth of it was sent back to Spain. As a final act of cruelty, Pizarro murdered Atahuallpa.

Within a period of ten years, thanks to Cortés and Pizarro, Spain had laid claim to all the riches of Central and South America. In addition, a silver mine was discovered on a fifteen-thousand-foot-high mountain in

In 1532, Spanish explorer Francisco Pizarro conquered the Incas in an effort to possess their riches.

Pieces of Eight and Today's Dollar Sign

Many pirate tales have used the term *pieces of eight* when referring to plundered treasure. Pieces of eight, or pesos, were the most famous coins associated with the New World. They were shipped back to Spain in massive quantities from mints in Mexico City; Lima, Peru; and Potosí, Bolivia. For more than one hundred years, pieces of eight were the standard coin used for trade in South and Central America and the West Indies.

Pieces of eight were roughly made coins that were sometimes almost square in shape, rather than round. One side of the coin showed the Spanish coat of arms. The other side had a design representing the two pillars of Hercules. Pieces of eight were so well known that the twin pillars on the coin eventually turned into the modern dollar sign. In 1644, one piece of eight was comparable to about $23 today.

modern-day Bolivia in 1545. The Spanish mined the ore and processed it into silver ingots using Native American and African slaves.

The silver was turned into coins called pieces of eight, which were shipped back to Spain at an amazing rate. Between 1596 and 1600, Spain imported treasure from the New World worth $774 million.

Plundering the Plunderers

Spain's discovery of vast riches did not go unnoticed. In 1523 Jean Fleury, a French privateer, sighted three heavily laden Spanish ships off the coast of Portugal. With a fleet of six ships, Fleury attacked and captured two of the Spanish treasure ships. The Frenchmen were astounded by what they found. They had stumbled upon tons of riches looted by Cortés. There were emeralds, topazes, gem-studded masks of gold, Aztec rings and helmets, and feathered cloaks. In addition, the Spanish were carrying 680 pounds of pearls and 500 pounds of gold dust in bags.

It was not long before Fleury's tale of plunder reached the highest courts of western Europe. By 1524 Francis I, the king of France, instructed all French sea captains to plunder Spanish treasure ships. This continued for forty years.

Letters of Marque

The Frenchmen had been given legal permission by their king to steal from the Spanish. It was granted by an official license known as a *letter of marque and reprisal* that gave these men, called privateers, the right to steal from ships belonging to enemy countries.

Letters of marque were not new in the 1500s—they had been issued for centuries. English king Henry III issued one of the first letters of marque in 1213. It read:

> Know ye that we have granted and given license to Adam Robernolt and William le Sauvage to annoy our enemies at sea or by land so that they shall share with us half their gain.[5]

Letters of marque sanctioned piracy and raised the status of the privateer above that of an outlaw, as long as the privateer attacked only foreign ships and continued to divide the loot with the Crown. A privateer with a letter of marque was protected by international law and could not be arrested or tried for piracy. But the system was open to abuse.

Some privateers, like other pirates, robbed from anyone and everyone.

The English Sea Dogs

The Spanish were alarmed by their losses at sea. Because single treasure ships were too vulnerable to French attack, the Spanish put together a convoy system of one hundred ships to transport their treasure back to Spain. This slowed down French attacks, which further declined as a result of civil war at home. In their place came a gradual rise of English pirates. By the late 1550s, the English had replaced the French as the principal plunderers in the Caribbean.

The first Englishman to challenge Spain's control over the New World trade was John Hawkins. Technically he was not a pirate or a privateer but a slave trader and a merchant

English slave trader and merchant John Hawkins was among the first foreigners to challenge Spain's domination of the New World.

whose trading voyages to the Spanish Main between 1563 and 1565 made him one of the richest men in England. Hawkins bought, sold, and stole products—and hundreds of African slaves—on the Spanish Main.

Spain did not tolerate the presence of foreign traders in the New World. The Spanish crown believed that it owned everything in all the waters and on all the lands of the Spanish Main. It regarded any foreign ship as guilty of trespassing. If New World products were on board a foreign ship, this would be considered proof of smuggling or poaching.

European traders like Hawkins were not easily dissuaded from the lucrative trade in the region. On June 4, 1568, twenty-eight-year-old Francis Drake, a cousin of Hawkins, sailed an advance vessel into a port in Colombia and asked for freshwater for Hawkins's fleet of trade ships. Spanish soldiers responded with a volley of cannon fire. Drake hastily withdrew.

The Spanish ordered their people to stop trading with the English. When Hawkins and Drake kept trying, the Spanish attacked their ships. During one particularly violent clash, the Spanish routed Hawkins's merchant ships, killing hundreds of English sailors. The two cousins barely made it back to England alive. After that defeat, Drake never stopped waging war on the Spanish.

The Deeds of Sir Francis Drake

Francis Drake was one of the greatest sea captains of the age. Sailing around the world at the age of thirty-one, he became internationally famous. The journey began in 1577 when Drake sailed from England to South America with five ships. He rounded the Straits of Magellan at the southern tip of South America and sailed up the continent's

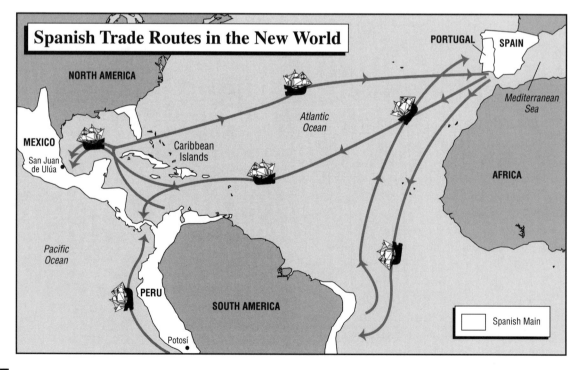

Spanish Trade Routes in the New World

west coast, robbing and plundering Spanish ships and settlements as he went. One Spanish ship yielded thousands of dollars worth of gold and seventeen hundred bottles of wine. Another gave up four thousand silver coins and a chest of gold.

Drake's most spectacular prize came on March 1, 1579, when he overtook the heavily armed Spanish treasure ship *Cacafuego*. Drake wrote in his diary about looting the ship:

> We found in her some fruit, sugars, meal and other victuals [food], and (that which was the special cause of her heavy and slow sailing) a certain quantity of jewels and precious stones, 13 chests of ryals of plate [silver coins], 80 pound weight in gold, 26 tons of uncoined silver, two very fair gilt silver drinking bottles, and the like trifles, valued at about 360,000 pesos. We gave the [captain] a little linen and the like, for these commodities; and at the end of six days we bade farewell and parted. He hastening somewhat lighter than before to Panama, we plying off to sea.[6]

In modern U.S. currency, the *Cacafuego*'s cargo would be worth about $108 million. It was one of the richest prizes of all time.

Drake's plundering of the *Cacafuego* alarmed Spanish authorities. Up and down the coast of South America, Spanish battleships hunted for Drake, but he had wisely headed west into the Pacific Ocean and sailed around the world via the Orient. Drake arrived back in Plymouth, England, on September 26, 1580—two years and nine months after he left.

Plundering the Spanish Main

Men like Fleury and Drake were the most famous privateers of their time. There were,

Francis Drake, the renowned privateer of the 1500s, boldly plundered Spanish treasure ships in the Caribbean.

however, thousands of pirates who operated in the Spanish Main with no authority from any government. With Aztec emeralds "as large as a man's fist," and "wondrously wrought gold works," many men believed that they had as much right to these riches as the Spanish. French buccaneer Louis Le Golif wrote:

> In America, fortune is to be found on the sea, where one must go to collect it. . . . I speak highly of the attractions of a life in which no day is like that which precedes or follows it, in which freedom is the rule and great riches can be quickly acquired.[7]

The great age of piracy, from Cortés to Drake, was played out in an area of the world known as the Spanish Main, so-called because the country of Spain laid claim to that vast area of the world. The term *Spanish Main* originally meant the mainland of Central and South America from Mexico to Peru. This

Spanish treasure ships were called galleons. They were loaded with gold, silver, and jewels. When galleons sailed home to Spain from the New World, they were the main target of pirates operating in the Caribbean Sea and Atlantic Ocean.

A typical galleon had two decks armed with 60 guns and weighed about 500 tons. The ship was about 35 feet wide and 125 feet long. There was a high, decorated structure at the stern (rear) of the ship with an observation nest built onto it.

Galleons hid their cargo chests of silver and gold in a packed treasure room on the lower deck. It was boarded up and guarded by soldiers during the homeward journey to the Spanish port of Seville.

The Spanish galleon carried enormous treasures of gold and silver from the New World back to Spain.

included the modern-day countries of Nicaragua, Costa Rica, and Panama. The Spanish Main later came to include the islands and waters of the Caribbean Sea, including Jamaica, Cuba, Santa Cruz (now Puerto Rico), Tortuga, Martinique, Barbados, Tobago, Trinidad, Grenada, and Hispaniola (now Haiti and the Dominican Republic). The peninsula of Florida was also under Spanish control. This area was virtually lawless, however, because Spain could not control such a large area from its capital more than two thousand miles away.

The Spanish Main was home to more than just large islands such as Jamaica. Hundreds of small islands are scattered throughout the warm, azure waters of the Caribbean. Some islands are nothing more than rocks sticking up above the water. Many of these lesser islands had never been inhabited by the Spanish. They dismissed them on their naval charts as *islas inútiles* or "useless islands." The islands were not useless, however, to sea rovers. They held small rivers and rocky inlets, which provided excellent hiding places for pirate ships. The pirates could simply lay in wait until a heavily loaded merchant ship sailed into view.

North American Pirate Places

During the eighteenth century, the eastern coast of North America joined the Spanish Main as fertile pirate hunting grounds. The English controlled this territory, from Massachusetts to Maryland and Virginia to the Carolinas. Trade from the areas was hampered by attacks from French, Spanish, and even American pirates.

All this piracy had a very negative effect on the New World economy. When pirate activity reached its peak in 1720, governors from Cuba to the Carolinas complained. Governor Johnson of South Carolina wrote to London in 1718:

> The unspeakable calamity this poor province suffers from pirates obliges me to inform your Lordship of it in order that his Majesty may know it and be induced to afford us the assistance of a frigate or two to cruise hereabouts upon them for we are continually alarmed and our ships taken to the utter ruin of our trade.[8]

The governor of Boston stated it more clearly: "The pirates still continue to rove the seas, and if a sufficient force is not sent to drive them off, our trade must stop."[9]

Why Poor Men Plundered

New World treasure ships were a powerful target that drew thousands of men (and a few women) to the lure of pirate riches. Pirates plied their trade in the Caribbean Sea for more than 250 years. They came out of nowhere, attacked their victims and looted their ships, then disappeared back into the sea from whence they came. This happened as often as six times a day for more than two centuries. But piracy was an outlaw profession punishable by death or imprisonment in most nations. Why, then, did so many leave behind the honest life to become thieves on the Spanish Main?

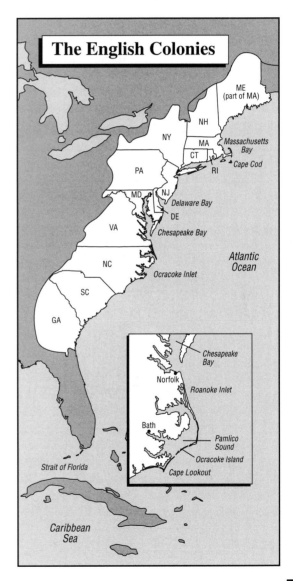

The English Colonies

The 1600s and 1700s were a time when a few people were very rich and the rest were extremely poor. Kings and queens spent their country's fortunes fighting costly wars. Common people struggled for daily survival. There was little or no work for many men. Economic realities pushed many farmers and tradesmen into the sailor's life, where there was always employment to be found on the ships.

In countries such as England, only the firstborn son could inherit the family farm or business. Other sons (and daughters) were forced to look elsewhere for a living. Many sons of poor farmers went to port cities to work on the docks and ships. Others were forced to work on ships by recruiters called press gangs. Press gangs conducted their recruitment by threat of injury. Sometimes unwilling enlistees were simply kidnapped.

For young men in their late teens life at sea offered the thrill of money and adventure. But these romantic illusions quickly dissolved under the rigors of a sailor's life. As a seaman's proverb attests, "Those who would go to the sea for pleasure would go to hell for a pastime."

Encapsulating many of the attractions, historian Ralph Davis offers his explanation of why men were drawn to the sea:

> To see the world, to get a good rate of pay, to get a good job of some sort at any price—these were the motives of those who went out to sea; perhaps some went willy-nilly, drunk, or unconscious.[10]

"Jail with a Chance of Being Drowned"

Happy and optimistic young men soon got a dose of hard reality once they boarded the merchant ships and went out to sea. Life-threatening accidents were common aboard sailing ships. Death lurked over every wave. Diseases such as consumption and scurvy raged on the ships. Food rations were small. Dozens of gales and hurricanes blew up every

Buccaneers battle sailors on the high seas. Many young men became pirates in search of fame, fortune, and adventure.

A pirate captain interviews a new recruit while members of his crew look on. Most pirate recruits were experienced seafarers who had served with the merchant marines or various navies.

summer. Discipline was brutal, and sailors who failed to obey commands were often killed. Wages were low, and sometimes sailors were not paid at all. Being stuck aboard a pitching, tossing ship for months on end was often compared with imprisonment. Dr. Samuel Johnson wrote: "Being in a ship is being in jail with a chance of being drowned. . . . A man in jail has more room, better food, and better company."[11]

For many, the only way out of the merchant marines was to join up with pirates. And join they did. A survey of English pirates in the Caribbean in 1720 showed that 98 percent were formerly seamen in the merchant marine or the British Royal Navy. Most volunteered to join the pirates when their merchant ships were captured.

When a merchant vessel was seized, the pirate captain would ask the seamen of the captured vessel who among them would serve under the skull and crossbones (pirate flag). Usually several men stepped forward. Sailors knew that employment on a pirate vessel was far better than on merchant or naval ships. Food was usually more plentiful, pay consid-

erably higher, and work shifts shorter. Skilled sailors such as sail makers and carpenters were desperately needed by the pirates to keep their ships in repair. If the craftsmen did not volunteer, they were usually kidnapped.

The Lure of Easy Money

With dozens of treasure-laden ships crisscrossing the oceans, there was no shortage of pirate bands to join. And when pirates swarmed aboard ships, they were looking for money, jewels, silver, and gold. Single coins such as the Spanish gold doubloon were worth seven weeks' pay for an honest sailor.

If they were lucky, a pirate crew could loot one ship and become rich beyond their wildest dreams. One raid on a Portuguese ship in 1721 netted each pirate of the sixty-man crew $4.3 million in jewels such as diamonds, emeralds, sapphires, rubies, and opals. When Henry Avery captured the Arab ship *Gang-i-Sawai*, the total haul was $400 million. Each of the 150 crew members received $2.5 million.

The average take was not so glamorous, however. Pirate Roger Dangerfield wrote of an attack on a French ship, "The pirates plundered the ship of fifty tons of iron, twenty-five pipes [barrels] of brandy, [and] several bales of linen."[12]

In general, the life of a pirate was almost as dirty and dangerous as life aboard a merchant ship. But pirates had their freedom, and many of them knew no other life.

Aristocrat Pirates

Not all pirates, however, were poor folks hoping to strike it rich. There were a few wealthy men—though not many—who were simply looking for adventure. Others were educated, upper-class men, called aristocrats, who had lost their fortunes and took up piracy to regain their wealth.

One of the more famous aristocrat pirates was an Englishman named Sir Henry Mainwaring, who was educated at the highly regarded Oxford College, where he studied law. In 1613 Mainwaring bought a ship and went to sea as a pirate. For two years, he plundered Spanish ships on the coast of Spain. In 1615 the aristocrat-turned-pirate went home to England and was granted a pardon. Mainwaring began a successful career as a naval commissioner and eventually became a member of Parliament, England's governing body. The Parliament pirate wrote several books on maritime subjects, one of them entitled *Of the Beginnings, Practices, and Suppression of Pirates.*

One of the oddest aristocrat pirates was Major Stede Bonnet, who lived comfortably in Barbados but was tired of the easy life. Bonnet fitted out a sloop with ten guns, assembled a crew of seventy men, and plundered ships along the coast of Virginia and

Major Stede Bonnet, one of the few aristocrat pirates, joined the dangerous profession when he grew bored with his life of leisure.

South Carolina. Bonnet's weakness was that he had no seafaring experience and thus could not command a ship. The famous pirate Blackbeard persuaded him to turn over his sloop to an experienced captain. The *Boston News Letter* reported in 1717: "Bonnet has been observed on Blackbeard's ship. He has no command [and] walks about in his morning gown, and then to his books of which he has a good library aboard."[13]

When Bonnet was arrested in South Carolina for pirating, his education was held against him at the trial. The judge wrote: "Bonnet was a Gentleman that has had the advantage of a liberal education, and being generally esteemed a Man of Letters."[14] Bonnet was hysterical when a death sentence was handed down. He wrote letters to the governor from prison but to no avail. He was hanged from the gallows on the Charleston waterfront.

The Rich Who Got Richer

While very few rich men would sail off on a pirate ship, quite a few were willing to finance pirates for a percentage of the loot. From the king of Spain, who financed Cortés and Pizarro, to wealthy English merchants, there was no shortage of people to aid pirates. Even middle-class working people hoped to get rich by pirate investment. Craftsmen such as tailors and carpenters supported pirates by buying stolen booty at low prices.

Successful voyages of plunder were profitable investments, with an average $100 return for every dollar invested. These investments were usually well-kept secrets—until the authorities found out. No one dreamt that Winchester butcher John Brexton was working hand in glove with pirate Edward Cooke until a gold-laden sea chest was carried into his house in broad daylight.

One lawyer, who himself worked with pirates, summed it up when he wrote:

> The generality [majority] of the people on the coasts are not unfriendly to the pirates. The men whose names appear in list after list of aiders and abettors needed little encouragement to assist pirates with provisions. Often these were barters for goods which labourers could not otherwise have afforded, such as wine, sugar, and spices.[15]

Like modern-day criminal activity, the promise of easy money corrupted the rich and the poor alike. For a few hundred years the pirate's life was a way to avoid society's rules. To see the world and plunder at will was a powerful draw. As pirate Black Bart once said, "It's a merry life—and a short one."[16]

The Captain and Crew

Except for a few rich men looking for adventure, pirates generally came from the lowest social classes. They were, as one official put it, "desperate rogues who could have little hope in life on shore."[17] These men owed allegiance to no one and were not bound to land by home and family.

In fact, most pirate ships would not take married men. The dangerous life of a sea robber was no place for a man longing for his wife and children. Proof of this is shown in a survey of eighteenth-century pirate trial statistics. Only 23 of the 521 sea robbers on trial were known to be married. On the other hand, a few pirates were married to several women at once, each of whom lived in a different port.

Pirates had many life experiences in common. This gave them a base of unity that might not have been shared by other occupations. And it affected the way pirates organized themselves in their daily activities.

Disciplined officers of the Royal Navy claimed that pirates had no regular command among them. But the pirates' order was simply different from the strict order of the merchant marines and navy; it was more democratic, placing authority in the hands of the crew as opposed to one central commander.

Who's Who on a Pirate Crew

Pirates took great joy in turning the rigid structure of the navy upside down. The pirate captain was elected by the crew and served at their pleasure. His command was only "in fighting, chasing, and being chased."[18] He could be dismissed for acts of cruelty or for refusing to pursue a potential prize. The captain was more of a figurehead than an authority figure, but he was usually considered one of the wisest men aboard ship.

A courageous captive refuses to become a pirate despite the demands of the pirate captain and his crew.

The quartermaster was second-in-charge after the captain, and his job was just as important. The quartermaster was in charge of distributing food and the stolen loot equally among the men. He also kept account books for the ship, led boarding parties onto enemy ships, and organized command parties for dangerous expeditions. When a ship was being looted, the quartermaster decided which plunder to keep, and what to leave behind. Many times a good quartermaster was eventually elected captain of a ship. On a less happy note, the quartermaster ordered punishments for minor offenses and took up the whip and administered all floggings.

Other crew members aboard a buccaneer ship paralleled those on a naval man-of-war. The lieutenant had no particular function except to replace the captain if he was killed. The sailing master was in charge of navigation and setting the sails. The boatswain, or bosun, was responsible for the ship's ropes and pulleys, called tackle. The gunner was in charge of guns and ammunition and overseeing the gun crews.

Other specialists were called "ship artists." They included the carpenter, sail maker, and surgeon. The surgeon was responsible for treating men for dozens of diseases. During battle he was in charge of amputations and dressing wounds. If there was no surgeon, the carpenter filled in—their tools, especially saws, were much the same.

The most popular men aboard ships were musicians. Usually kidnapped from other ships, the musicians were spared torture because of their ability to entertain the often-bored pirate crew. The bandsmen were called upon to play a jig or a hornpipe at a pirate dance, or to serenade the pirates as they took their meals. During battle the band was ordered to play nautical tunes and war music on their drums, bagpipes, and trumpets.

Of course, every pirate ship was different, but in reading history, a general order becomes clear. As revolutionaries from society's rules, pirates tended to share their riches, enforce discipline fairly, and assign authority by vote. These traits were noticeably missing from most of seventeenth- and eighteenth-century society.

Dividing the Spoils

The buccaneers of Tortuga began to call themselves the Brethren of the Coast around 1640. To acquire membership in this democratic institution, a man vowed to sign a paper called the *chasse-partie*, or charter-party. This charter described the conditions under which the pirates were to sail. Signers of the paper were known by only their first names—last names were taboo. Among the buccaneers, this code was more important than any national laws.

Before sailing, buccaneers held council aboard ship. Unless one of the men owned the ship, pirates selected their captain from among themselves. The pirates decided where to seek provisions such as food and water. They determined where to sail to "seek their desperate fortunes." And they listed the exact share of the hoped-for booty each pirate was to receive. No one was paid unless a fortune could be found. This rule was known as "no prey, no pay." After a cruise was finished, each pirate was on his own until he signed on to another *chasse-partie*.

John Esquemeling, also known as Alexander Exquemelin, was a former slave who sailed with buccaneers for many years. In 1642 he wrote a bloodthirsty account of their methods, which became a best-seller and was translated into several languages. The book, *The Buccaneers of America*, is still in

Pirate crews operated on a "no prey, no pay" rule: If no treasure was seized, no one was paid. Here, successful buccaneers divide their spoils.

print today. In it, Esquemeling describes how pirates divided their booty:

> In the first place . . . they mention how much the Captain ought to have for his ship. Next the salary of the carpenter, or shipwright, who careened [cleaned], mended and rigged the vessel. Afterwards for provisions and victualling [food] they draw out of the same common stock. Also a competent salary for the surgeon and his chest of medicaments [medicine].[19]

Whatever remained of the booty was divided into shares and distributed among the crew. The captain got five or six times more than the ordinary crewman. The lowest-ranked boys—sometimes only twelve or thirteen years old—got only half a share. The pirate who sighted a treasure ship won an extra share. Musicians, whose loud and raucous music served to urge on the pirates and unnerve the enemy, also received a greater share of the booty.

Sailing was dangerous work. That is why the pirate's code of conduct specified compensation to those who were injured carrying out their assignments. John Esquemeling spells it out in his book:

> Lastly, they stipulate in writing what recompense or reward each one ought to have, that is either wounded or maimed in his body, suffering the loss of any limb, by that voyage. Thus they order the loss of a right arm 600 pieces of eight, or six slaves; for the loss of a left arm 500 pieces of eight, or five slaves; for a right leg 500 pieces of eight, or five slaves; a left leg 400 pieces of eight or 4 slaves; for an eye or a finger of the hand 100 pieces of eight or one slave.[20]

Pirate Punishment

Most men who became pirates believed that rules were made to be broken. But a pirate who broke the code of conduct after signing it was subjected to harsh punishment. Before the punishment could be carried out, however, the entire crew had to vote on whether it was justified. Buccaneers were violently opposed to unjust punishments. As pirate Francis Kennedy stated: "Having suffered formerly from the ill-treatment of their officers [in the navy, pirates] provided carefully against such an evil."[21]

The most famous pirate punishment—walking the plank—was never practiced. Sending a man overboard to a watery death was the invention of author Charles Elms in his 1837 book *The Pirate's Own Book*. That punishment would be a quick and easy death compared to the real punishments that rule-breaking buccaneers suffered.

A freebooter's worst punishment was marooning. The offender was simply put ashore on a deserted island far from land with no

The Pirate's Code of Conduct

Popular myth conceives of pirates as driven only by greed. But pirates' lives were governed by strict rules and regulations. One of the earliest authorities on pirate life was Captain Charles Johnson, who wrote a book in 1724 called A General History of the Robberies and Murders of the Most Notorious Pirates. *Johnson's book printed a code of conduct that pirates had to sign before every mission. The articles were written out and "all swore to 'em upon a hatchet, for want of a Bible." Excerpted here from David Cordingly and John Falconer's* Pirate Fact and Fiction, *these codes varied from ship to ship but were essentially the same for most pirate crews.*

"The Articles Of Piracy:

ARTICLE 1: Every man shall obey civil command; the captain shall have one full share and a half in all prizes. The Master, Carpenter, Boatswain, and Gunner shall have one share and quarter.

ARTICLE 2: If any man shall offer to run away, or keep any secret from the Company, he shall be maroon'd with one bottle of powder, one bottle of Water, one small Arm, and shot [bullets].

ARTICLE 3: If any Man shall steal any Thing in the Company, or game, to the value of a piece of Eight, he shall be Marroon'd or shot.

ARTICLE 4: That a man that shall strike another, whilst these Articles are in force, shall receive Moses's Law (that is 40 Stripes [of a whip] lacking one) on the bare Back.

ARTICLE 5: That Man that shall snap his Arms, or smoak Tobacco in the Hold, without cap to his Pipe, or carry a candle lighted without lanthorn, shall suffer the same Punishment as in the former Article.

ARTICLE 6: If any man shall lose a joint in time of Engagement, shall have 400 Pieces of Eight: if a limb, 800.

ARTICLE 7: If at any time you meet with a prudent Woman, that Man that offers to meddle with her, without her Consent, shall suffer Death."

Pirate Bartholomew Roberts, or Black Bart, set out some rules of his own that required: "no person to game at cards or dice for money," "the lights and candles to be put out at eight o'clock at night," "the musicians to have rest on Sabbath day, but the other six days and nights none, without special favor," and robbery between pirates was punishable by "slitting the ears and nose of him that was guilty."

food and very little drinking water. Only a few pirates survived marooning. Pirates were not usually marooned on large islands covered with lush plant life, as portrayed in books and movies. Quite the contrary, these islands were usually nothing more than bald sandbars that might disappear underwater at high tide, leaving the pirate in water up to his neck.

A typical marooned pirate was left with very few provisions. Captain John Phillips allowed a marooned pirate "one bottle of [gun] powder, one bottle of water, one small arm [pistol], and shot."[22] But the unlucky buccaneer had no way of cooking food or keeping warm. After the drinking water was gone, the pirate was often left with nothing but undrinkable seawater. The reason the pirate was left with a pistol was so that he could take his own life when the situation became dire. Marooning was the worst type of punishment, reserved for murderers, rapists, bad captains, and thieves.

It was unlikely that anyone would actually rescue a maroon. An honest sea captain would assume that anyone wandering a desert island was a pirate and so would leave him there, or worse clap him in leg irons and take him to shore to be hanged.

One pirate who thrived after marooning was Alexander Selkirk, who lived on an island off the coast of Chile from 1705 to 1709. The pirate was sick of arguments onboard and actually asked to be marooned. Left on one of the Juan Fernandes Islands, Selkirk had a good supply of wild pigs and goats along with freshwater. He passed the time by taming wild cats and goats and teaching them to dance. When he was found by rescuers, ragged and dressed in goatskins, Selkirk at first refused to leave his island home.

Unruly pirates are forced to walk the plank in this scene from The Pirate's Own Book. *Author Charles Elms invented the now famous—but entirely inaccurate—punishment for his 1837 book.*

A marooned pirate sits on the shores of a desert island. Without food, water, or shelter, marooned pirates were destined to perish.

Flogging

Another popular pirate punishment was flogging with a whip called a cat-o'-nine-tails. The cat was a particularly nasty whip with nine lengths of cord, each with a knot on the end. It could inflict horrible pain and injury. A pirate to be flogged was forced to first make the cat-o'-nine-tails that was to be used on him.

Pirates who committed the most serious offenses were said to receive Moses' Law, which means forty lashes minus one, or thirty-nine lashes. The term is from the Bible, which determined under the Old Testament that thirty-nine lashes are just and fair. It was considered "unchristian" to flog someone more than that. In truth, thirty-nine lashes was enough to kill a man. Quite often the captain or quartermaster would mete out fewer lashes depending on the crime. The British Royal Navy allowed only twelve lashes.

Pirate Crew Characteristics

During the early eighteenth century, there were about two thousand to twenty-four hundred pirates operating on the Spanish Main at any one time. With such a relatively small group, it is probable that many men served together at one time or another. Sometimes pirate ships would meet at sea and join together for plundering.

The pirate's code of conduct acted as a common bond among men who might not have a single country in common. A pirate ship could be abuzz with five different spoken languages. Trial and court records show pirates to be of many different nationalities and races. On a single ship there might be rogues from England, Wales, Scotland, Ireland, Spain, France, Italy, Portugal, the Netherlands, Greece, and Scandinavia. There were also escaped African slaves, African Americans, Native Americans, and people of mixed races.

Some pirate captains welcomed runaway African slaves into their crews. Because of their fearless fighting skills, some black pirates made up the vanguard of the pirates' attack party. More than half of Edward Condent's boarding party was black. Blacks and men of mixed races, or mulattos, were present on almost every pirate ship. Sixty of Blackbeard's hundred-man crew were black.

Young and Old Pirates

There were very few older pirates. Some pirate captains were in their thirties or forties, but the average pirate was about twenty-seven years old. Sailors generally joined the navy at seventeen, and a sailor's life was often a short one. Governor Francis Nicholson of Virginia, quoted in The Pirates *by Douglas Botting, gives a vivid description of some outlaw British pirates in 1699. Wanted for plundering were the following:*

"Tee Wetherley, short, very small, blind in one eye, about 18; Thomas Hughs, tall, lusty, rawboned, long visage, swarthy, about 28; Thomas Jameson, cooper, Scottish, tall, meagre, sickly looking, large black eyes, 20; William Griffith, short, well set, broad face, darkest hair, about 30; John Loyd, ordinary stature, rawboned, very pale, dark hair, remarkably deformed in the lower eyelid; William Saunders, of ordinary stature, wellset, fresh-colored, black hair, about 15; Thomas Simpson, short and small, much squint-eyed, about 10 years of age."

Ages are known for 117 pirates active between 1716 and 1726. They range from 17 to 50 years old, with an average age of 27. The age distribution was almost identical to the merchant marines and Royal Navy.

Pirate captain William Lewis wrote of "40 able Negroe sailors," while Oliver la Bouche had a ship that was "half French, half Negro." Free blacks and runaway slaves "went off to join pirates who did not seem too concerned about color differences."[23] Pirates were also unconcerned about nationalities—when asked where they came from the standard answer was "from the sea."

Pirates' Fashions

Regardless of their national origin, crew members made statements about their private affiliation by the way they looked and dressed. Countless paintings and movies portray pirates dressed in silk, velvet, gold, and fine leather. While some pirates did dress in gaudy and outrageous fashions, most pirate garb was drab and practical. When at sea, the average pirate wore pants and a close-fitting sleeveless jacket called a jerkin. The garments were made from the rough canvas also used for sails. These clothes were tough and durable. Pirates sometimes wore short jackets over checkered shirts, waistcoats, and loosely tied scarves or kerchiefs around their necks. Captains of pirate ships might wear the plundered clothing of naval officers or merchant sea captains. When going into battle, pirates donned clothing coated with a dark, sticky substance called pitch that was made from coal, wood, or oil. Pitch helped deflect the thrust of a sword.

Once onshore, many pirates tended to make up for their dull work clothes by donning the colorful dress of rich gentlemen. Buccaneers traipsed about in silver- or gold-buckled high-heeled shoes, tricornered hats, embroidered silks, satins, velvet, and lace. The garments tended to be brightly colored, but mismatched, as they were usually stolen at different times and places. Some even wore powdered wigs and face powder, which was fashionable with the aristocrats of the day. They also exaggerated the mannerisms of rich men.

Flaunting his ill-gotten wealth, a buccaneer might be found wearing rings, earrings, elaborate pendants, pearls, heavy gold chains, diamonds, emeralds, and even crosses stolen from Catholic priests.

Captain Charles Johnson described the appearance of Black Bart (Bartholomew Roberts) in 1724 as the pirate boarded his captured ship:

> Roberts himself made a gallant figure at the time of the engagement, being dressed in a rich crimson damask waistcoat and breeches, a red feather in his hat, a gold chain around his neck, with a diamond cross hanging to it, a sword in his hand and two pair of pistols, hanging at the end of a silk sling, flung over his shoulders.[24]

The dress and appearance of a pirate depended on his or her luck at plunder. Some motley crews were dressed only in rags, while successful pirates like Black Bart resembled the richest men of their day.

Women Pirates

The violent, brutal pirate trade was dominated by these would-be gentlemen, but there were a few well-known women pirates. Anne Bonny, born in 1700, was one of the most famous. Her father was a well-to-do lawyer, but the beautiful, red-headed girl spent her teens hanging out on the tough docks of Charles Town (Charleston), South Carolina, where hundreds of pirates plied their trade. When Anne was only fifteen, she married a pirate named James Bonny and moved to New Providence, a notorious haven for pirates in the Bahamas.

Anne soon left her husband and fell in love with Jack Rackam, known as Calico Jack.

A well-dressed sea captain shakes hands with a one-legged pirate. Armed with pistols and sporting a peg leg, this pirate dons the typical attire of a sea rogue.

Dressed as a man, with a pistol in one hand and a sword in the other, Anne, with Rackam, stole the fastest sloop in Nassau harbor. Along with a kidnapped crew, the two soon became the scourge of the Caribbean, plundering traders and even fishing boats.

One of their crew members was a handsome young Dutch boy to whom Bonny took a liking. She soon found out that the youth was neither Dutch nor a boy, but an Englishwoman named Mary Read.

Mary Read was born in Plymouth, England, around 1690. Her mother dressed her as a boy from the time she was a small child so she could claim an inheritance when she was thirteen. (In those days, only boys could inherit

Blackbeard's Fashion Statement

Edward Teach, better known as Blackbeard, was one of the most fearsome—and famous—pirates on the Spanish Main. He roamed the Caribbean in 1718 with three hundred men on his ship Queen Anne's Revenge. *Blackbeard, originally from Bristol, England, was known for his shocking appearance as well as for his diabolical deeds. The most memorable description of Blackbeard comes from Captain Charles Johnson's* A General History of the Robberies and Murders of the Most Notorious Pirates, *published in 1724. Johnson, here excerpted from Douglas Botting's* The Pirates, *describes Blackbeard:*

"Captain Teach assumed the cognomen [nickname] of Black-beard, from that large quantity of hair, which, like a frightful meteor, covered his whole face, and frightened America more than any comet that has appeared there [in] a long time.

The beard was black, which he suffered to grow of an extravagant length; as to breadth, it came up to his eyes; he was accustomed to twist it with ribbons, in small tails, and turn them about his ears: in time of action, he wore a sling over his shoulders, with three brace of pistols, hanging in holsters like bandoliers; and stuck lighted matches [hempen cord that had been soaked in saltpeter and limewater that produced a thick black smoke around the pirate's head] under his hat, which appearing on each side of his face, his eyes naturally looked fierce and wild, made him altogether such a figure, that imagination cannot form an idea of a fury, from Hell, to look more frightful."

Blackbeard's personality matched his appearance. He drank huge quantities of rum and was said to be married to fourteen women. Blackbeard's performance at sea was less impressive than his appearance. His reign of terror lasted less than two years before he was killed in battle.

A romantic painting depicts the countenance of the dreaded pirate Blackbeard, renowned for his outlandish appearance and fearsome personality.

Infamous Anne Bonny began her career as a pirate at age fifteen. Soon afterwards, Bonny was plundering the Caribbean in search of treasure.

land or money.) Mary became a servant—not a maid or cook, but a footboy. But "here she did not live long, for growing bold and strong, and having also a roving mind, she entered herself on board a man-of-war."[25]

Mary fell in love with an officer who, when he discovered she was a woman, "was much surprised . . . and not a little pleased."[26] The young couple married, but when Mary's husband died she was forced once again to earn a living. She dressed as a man and joined the Dutch navy. On a voyage to the Carib-

bean, the ship was attacked by Bonny and Calico Jack. Mary signed the pirate articles and joined up with the freebooters.

One day in 1720 the two women, again dressed as men, attacked a merchant ship off Jamaica. An alert female passenger, Dorthy Thomas, said, "By the largeness of their breasts, I believed them to be women."[27]

A month later, Calico Jack and Bonny and Read were captured by authorities, though not without a fight. When an English naval sloop surprised them, Jack and the crew had

Mary Read plunges a sword through the belly of her opponent. Disguised as a man, Read enlisted in the Dutch navy and later joined forces with Anne Bonny and Jack Rackam.

been drinking, and were too drunk to fight back. But Read and Bonny flew at the navy men with pistols firing and cutlasses and axes flailing. When Bonny realized that they were outnumbered, she turned on her fellow pirates lying in a drunken stupor. She killed one crewmate and wounded several others, screaming at the cowardly pirates to "come up and fight like men!"[28]

At their trial, Read and Bonny were sentenced—like the other pirates—to death. When asked by the judge if they had anything to say, the women said, "Milord, we plead our bellies." Both women were pregnant. The judge immediately stayed the order of execution. As Calico Jack went to his death, Bonny yelled at him: "If you had fought like a man, you need not have been hanged like a dog!"[29]

Mary Read died of fever in prison before her child was born. No further records exist of Anne Bonny, but legends say that she was released from prison on the promise that she would quit the pirate business and leave the Caribbean. Rumor has it that she lived to be ninety years old and spent her days on a vast southern plantation with nothing but female finery in her stunning wardrobe.

The attitudes of Anne Bonny and Mary Read mirrored those of other pirates during the seventeenth and eighteenth centuries who took society's rules and turned them upside down. Pirates invented their own way of dressing, their own way of living, and their own way of governing themselves. In this, the buccaneers were ahead of their time. Democratic rule among nonpirates did not exist until after the American Revolution in 1776.

3 Sailing over the Bounty Main

Pirates sailed several kinds of ships that were popular in the eighteenth century. The crews required that their ships be fast, well armed, and agile. Pirates prized speed and power so they could easily overrun cargo-heavy merchant ships. Agility and firepower also aided pirates in evading and defending themselves against the roving fleets of the British Royal Navy, whose light, fast ships were crewed with heavily armed, trained fighters.

Outlaw pirates had no shipyards to provide them with crafts customized to their needs. Instead they plied their trade in a series of stolen merchant ships, which they altered to serve their purposes.

Pirates and Their Ships

When a pirate band first formed, the beginnings could be quite modest. Twenty or thirty men might buy a canoe, board the first fishing boat they came across, kill the fishermen or put them onshore, and sail off with their vessel. Other times the pirates borrowed vessels or had them provided by financial backers. The backers would get one-third of the loot upon the completion of the voyage.

For pirates, different ships had different advantages, and disadvantages. One of the most desirable ships was the three-masted square-rigger. Although not as swift as other ships, the square-rigger was huge—110 feet in length and weighing 350 tons. The ship was capable of long voyages and could hold 150 to 200 pirates, along with 20 cannons and numerous other guns. The large cargo hold of the square-rigger could be filled with plenty of stolen loot. And such a large ship was better for riding out the storms and hurricanes that are common in the Caribbean. Square-riggers served pirates well on long-distance journeys on the Pirate's Round—from the Caribbean, up the North American coast to Newfoundland, across the Atlantic, then down into Africa and beyond.

The single-masted sloop was the most common ship used by buccaneers. The sloop could carry seventy-five pirates and fourteen cannons. They were the most nimble of ships and were built in Jamaica or the Bahamas. Their fairly shallow draft made sloops perfect for winding through channels and sounds. Sloops were remarkable for the extremely long, stout pole, called a bowsprit, that extended in front of the ship. This allowed the sloop to mount a parade of canvas sails, making it the most maneuverable of ships. Sloops could outsail most other crafts that pursued them.

The buccaneer workhorse ship was the brigantine. It was also the ship chosen for combat on the open seas. Brigantines were characterized by their 2 masts that held numerous square sails in various combinations. This allowed the ship to sail into the wind or quarter to it. The vessel was 80 feet long and, at 150 tons, was large enough for 10 cannons and a crew of 100.

The mighty brigantine, workhorse of the pirates. The brigantine's enormity allowed it to carry ten cannons and a crew of one hundred, making it especially valuable during combat.

The schooner was a less popular ship. With two masts, the schooner had a narrow frame. Its great advantage was speed—up to 11 knots (about 13 miles per hour). At 100 tons, the schooner was large enough to carry 75 buccaneers to man its 8 cannons and 4 small-caliber swivel guns. Another advantage was its extremely shallow draft—only 5 feet. This enabled the schooner to maneuver in shallow waters where other ships could not follow.

Little Boats and Merchant Ships

While the majority of pirate attacks were made by sailing ships, sometimes buccaneers would attack in small, open boats. Pirates who had not yet stolen a large craft, or were look-ing for the element of surprise, occasionally rowed up to their victims in stolen canoes. These canoes, dug out of large tree trunks, were popular with West Indies fishermen. Large canoes were called *piragua* in Spanish or *periangers* in English. They could hold 25 men and were either rowed or fitted with a sail. A smaller version was about 23 feet long and could hold 5 or 6 pirates.

The main pirate target was the merchant ship, a 3-masted, square-sailed monster that weighed in at 280 tons. With fewer than 10 cannons and a crew of 19 men, merchant ships were easy prey as they slowly crossed the seas. To save on an owner's expenses, merchant ships had small crews and were lightly armed. Nineteen merchant marines were no match for a ship holding 200 screaming pirates armed to the teeth. Immediate surrender was the only option.

Customizing a Ship

The armaments of a pirate ship were less important than its seaworthiness. Guns could always be added later. When pirates stole a ship, they typically found a secluded bay where they could remake the ship for their own purposes.

When Welsh pirate Black Bart captured the frigate called the *Onslow* in 1721, he set about

> making such alterations as might fit her for a Sea Rover, pulling down her bulkheads, and making her flush, so that she became, in a respect, as complete a ship for their purpose as they could have found; and they continued to her [applied to the ship] the name of the *Royal Fortune* and mounted her with 40 guns.[30]

By pulling down the bulkheads (inner compartments) and other walls, the pirates made a large open space for working the guns. By "making her flush," the pirates removed cabins on the deck, which gave them an uncluttered platform on which to fight. Having cleared the deck, Bart's men transferred guns from their old ship, adding them to the *Royal Fortune*'s existing guns. Carpenters cut holes in the ship, called gunports, for such a purpose. The result was a battle-ready ship that could easily pulverize any merchant ship.

Every ship had to have a name. And the names pirates gave their ships were as colorful as the pirates themselves. The bow and

Using small boats to avoid detection, pirates survey anchored ships in an African port.

stern were usually decorated with the word *Revenge*. For those of whom revenge was not enough, there was *Revenge's Revenge* and *Queen Anne's Revenge*. Other expressive names included *Defiance, Bravo, Adventure Galley, Sudden Death*, and *Flying Dragon*.

Navigating the Seven Seas

For pirates to thrive, they had to fight better than their victims. But they also had to outsail them on the open seas and outwit them to capture them. And they had to do it all on the treacherous reefs and shoals of the Caribbean. It took a combination of common sense, knowledge, skill, and luck for pirates to find their way.

Navigation techniques were quite primitive in the seventeenth and eighteenth centuries. Pirates had navigation instruments to measure latitude (how far north or south they were), but there was no way of accurately reading longitude (east to west). This is why explorers such as Columbus had no idea where they were located at sea or when they would reach land.

Pirates had to position themselves along known trade routes or else they were just floundering at sea. These routes, in the days of sailing, were along prevailing winds. Skilled navigators were the most important men on a ship. Using an instrument called a backstaff, a ship's master could measure the altitude of the midday sun. This meant that a captain could know within approximately seven miles where he was in a north-south direction.

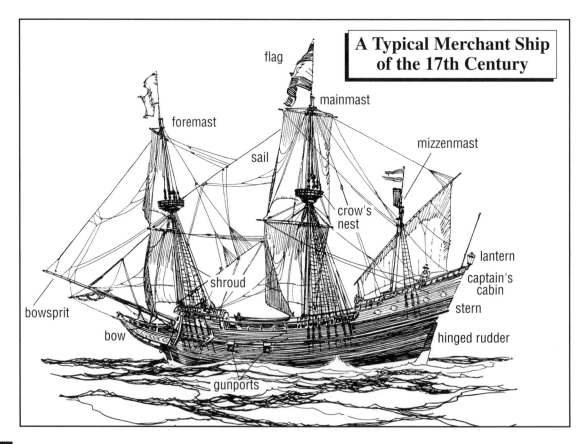

A Typical Merchant Ship of the 17th Century

flag

mainmast

foremast

mizzenmast

sail

crow's nest

lantern

captain's cabin

shroud

stern

bowsprit

hinged rudder

bow

gunports

Maps, Charts, and Waggoners

Beautifully drawn charts and maps were also useful, but many of these were inaccurate. They were worth their weight in gold because they gave the general shape of the coastlines and the general positions of the islands in a specific region. Many, however, tended to overestimate the size of the Atlantic Ocean. This could be a dangerous error as a mistake of ten degrees longitude translated into six hundred miles traveling distance.

Books of charts were called waggoners. They were among the prize items a pirate could steal. Bartholomew Sharp seized a waggoner of South America from a Spanish ship in 1681. He wrote in his journal:

> I took a Spanish manuscript of prodigious value—it describes all the ports, roads, harbours, bays, sands, rocks and risings of the land, and instructions how to work a ship into any port or harbour.[31]

These charts were valued not only by pirates but governments as well. Sharp was put on trial for piracy by England; he had stolen 4 million pesos from the Spanish, destroyed twenty-five of their ships, and killed two hundred Spanish sailors. (England and Spain were not at war at the time so Sharp's plundering was illegal.) The maps Sharp had stolen saved his life. They had such value that after Sharp presented them to King Charles II, he was set free. Sharp had rescued the maps seconds before they were thrown overboard by the Spanish, who would have rather destroyed them than let them fall into foreign hands.

Flying the Flag of Fear

As sailors and pirates navigated their way through the seas, they needed to identify

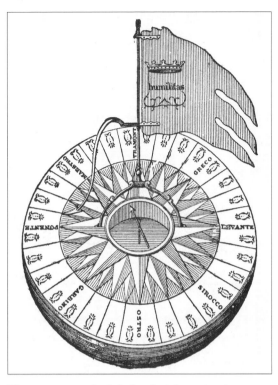

The compass, which helped with navigation, was an essential tool aboard pirate vessels.

The mariner's astrolabe, used to determine latitude, was developed in the sixteenth century. Compasses, sundials, lunar charts, and calendars were used to determine times of high and low tides. The compass was perhaps the most important tool, allowing navigators to head the ship in the desired direction. At night the octant was used to measure stars to approximate a ship's location. The telescope was nicknamed the "bring 'em near," and was invented in 1690. Telescopes helped a captain keep land in sight and also spy a possible victim or navy ship.

Many of these instruments were handcrafted of finely wrought brass, ivory, silver, and gold. These instruments of navigation, along with maps, charts, and books, were the first things pirates went after when they invaded a ship.

Despite their inaccuracies, hand-drawn maps were invaluable resources for sailors and pirates alike. This map shows the Gulf of Mexico and the Caribbean, replete with sea monsters and sailing ships.

other ships that they sighted. Flags flying on ships served to communicate captains' nationalities. In the days before radio and Morse code signaling, the only way ships could recognize each other was by flags. The traditional black pirate flag with a skull and crossbones spoke the universal language of fear to all who saw it.

The skull and crossbones, also known as the Jolly Roger or the death's-head, had been used in Europe since medieval times. Ship captains in those times used the symbol in their log books to indicate the death of a sailor. Pirates adopted the symbol around 1700.

By 1730, the Jolly Roger was standard equipment for any pirate ship. There are different theories as to how the flag was named. One is that it is an English pronunciation of the French term *jolie rouge*, used to describe the red or bloody flag that was also a pirate symbol. Another suggests that it was named after Ali Raja, a pirate operating in the Indian Ocean. The third is that the flag was named for "Old Roger," an English nickname for the devil.

Although the skull and crossbones has been associated with pirates for hundreds of years, it was only one of the many symbols used by pirates. Other images included blazing cannonballs, hearts dripping blood, hourglasses, spears, whole skeletons, and cutlasses. Red flags were used at least as often as black, and a plain red flag was the most terrifying. It meant no mercy would be shown—death to all who laid eyes upon it. Often the flag would contain three symbols that meant death, violence, and limited time. For instance, the skull and crossbones (death) would be emblazoned next to an arm with a sword (violence) followed by an hourglass (limited time). When on a red flag, it told the quarry to surrender without a fight or a bloody death would follow.

Some pirate captains had their own symbols. Blackbeard's black flag showed a horned skeleton holding an hourglass in one hand and a spear in the other. The spear was pointed to a bloody red heart. Bartholomew Roberts showed a pirate toasting a wine glass with a skeleton holding a spear. Calico Jack's flag showed a leering skull over two crossed cutlasses.

Pirate flags were usually sewn together by the ship's sail maker or any other member of the crew who could wield a needle and thread. There were also seamstresses who

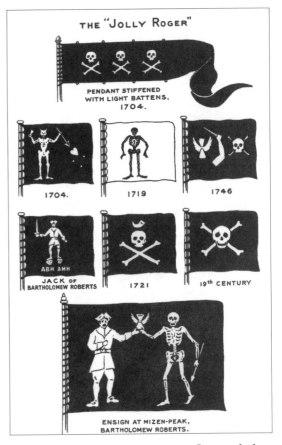

Examples of terror-inspiring pirate flags, including the banners of Blackbeard (1704) and Black Bart.

worked for pirates. One woman, a sail maker's widow, made pirate flags on New Providence Island and traded them for brandy.

Rigors of Life at Sea

The old Jolly Roger gives a romantic picture of a swashbuckling sailor's life at sea. But pirate life could be more accurately described as days of hard work and boredom followed by hours of terror when navigating a storm or attacking a ship.

Pirates needed to work constantly at the rigors of sailing. The sea is a perilous place, so pirates needed to tend watches, post lookouts, check water depths, and navigate accurately. In heavy weather, pirates were wet and cold for days on end. In calm weather, there might be nothing to do for weeks but mend sails, eat, and drink.

Most pirates had weathered, scarred faces, burnt brown from the scorching tropical sun. They were liable to have missing fingers and limbs from handling rough ropes and sails in heavy weather. Months of keeping their balance on the heaving decks of ships gave them a rolling kind of walk.

But life was still much easier for a pirate than for a merchant sailor. Pirate crews were not driven by ship owners to make the fastest possible crossings. And pirates operated with much larger crews. A merchant ship of one hundred tons might have twelve men aboard, while a similar pirate ship would have eighty or more. Pirates therefore had more men to heave the anchor, haul the ropes, set the sails, work the pumps, load and unload, man the boats, and go ashore for food and water.

"Kenneling Like Hounds"

No matter the size of the crew, life aboard an eighteenth-century wooden sailing vessel was severe. Ships were dark, damp, cheerless places. They reeked of rotting wood, human filth, bilge water, and rotten meat. Ships leaked regardless of the weather, and in heavy weather, water poured in belowdecks soaking everything. Men suffered from heat and cold. Their clothes were constantly wet, and the work of hauling ropes and sails and manning pumps rarely stopped. When work ceased at night, a sailor might have a single candle and a sopping wet blanket for comfort.

The larger crews on pirate ships had an advantage when it came to work. But so many

pirates in such a small place made daily life hellish. Sometimes 250 men lived in an area 127 feet long and 40 feet wide. They slept side by side on the floor, packed together in the hold, or as one captured captain put it, "kenneling like hounds on the deck."[32]

The all-male makeup of a pirate community cultivated a macho image. This was demonstrated by hard drinking, swearing, and casual cruelty. Phillip Ashton, who was captured by pirates in 1722, describes the experience:

> I soon found that any death was preferable to being linked with such a crew of vile miscreants [criminals], to whom it was a sport to do mischief, where prodigious drinking, monstrous cursing and swearing, hideous blasphemies, and open defiance of Heaven, and contempt of hell itself, was constant employment, unless when sleep . . . abated the noise and revellings.[33]

Pestilence and Disease

With so many men in so small a place, disease was rampant. Pirates tried to keep it at bay, washing down their decks with vinegar and saltwater. Some even slopped the decks with stolen French brandy or other alcohol. Belowdecks, sailors burned pitch or brimstone. But nothing could stop the infestations of vermin during a long voyage.

Pirate ships, like their merchant counterparts, were breeding grounds for beetles, cockroaches, fleas, and rats, who scurried throughout the hold. During a long voyage, it was not unusual for a captain to lose half his crew to disease. Typhus and typhoid were rampant. Sailors who lacked fresh fruit fell victim to scurvy. They suffered from malaria, dysentery, and yellow fever. Even successful pirate ships were crawling with pestilence. Author A. E. Mason describes the appalling conditions found on the ship of Francis Drake:

A hundred men would be crowded into a ship that today would not now be allowed to carry more than twenty. They were young men and boys for the most part, and for the most part, they died young men and boys. Disease set in inevitably. Scurvy, typhus and meningitis ran through the ship like the black plague. There were no lavatories, no refrigerators, no cold-storage rooms. Their food crawled with worms, their water rotted, they died like flies. Drake himself, who had survived many long voyages, finally succumbed to dysentery on board his ship.[34]

Sexually transmitted diseases such as syphilis were another pirate curse. Upon boarding a vessel, pirates were often most interested in ransacking medicine chests for syphilis treatments and other remedies.

Drunken pirates become belligerent aboard their crowded ship. Pirate vessels were typically overcrowded and infested with disease and vermin.

Food

Sometimes a pirate ship would carry a small store of good food called a petty tally to feed dying men. This would consist of bacon, beef tongues, marmalade, currants, and almonds. But pirates who were to live were not so lucky.

Historians agree that all sailors' food was horrible. The water stank, the meat and fish were rotten, and the biscuits were infested with large, black-headed maggots. Some men could bring themselves to eat only in the dark so they would not have to gaze upon such unsightly fare. But at least navy and merchantmen had food.

Thirst and starvation were a pirate's constant companions. Pirates had no predictable method of obtaining food or water. They had to change course often, hide in remote areas of distant oceans, and wait until a food-laden merchantman came into view. Sometimes the winds died down leaving a ship drifting aimlessly, unable to move. These problems often put pirate crews on desperately short rations.

Turtles, Fish, Birds, and Satchels

Buccaneers were usually able to live off the sea's bounty. Sea turtles were plentiful and slow on land—easy for a pirate to catch. Turtles could be kept alive aboard ship to provide fresh meat when necessary. Their soft-shelled eggs were a delicacy.

Pirates kept chickens aboard their ships and called their fresh eggs "cackle-fruit." Hard-baked biscuits of flour and water were

This nineteenth-century illustration depicts sword-wielding pirates attacking a ship. Buccaneers often waylaid merchant ships to obtain much needed food and supplies.

known as "hardtack" because they were so tough. Scurvy, which is caused by lack of vitamin C, was kept at bay by eating limes.

On islands, birds and small animals had not yet learned to be afraid of humans, so they were easy prey for pirates. Islands also teemed with wild goats, cattle, and pigs introduced by the Spanish. If none were to be found, the hungry men ate whatever they could find, including monkeys and snakes. And of course there was fish and other seafood. Along the coast of South America, Captain Sharp's buccaneers were eating "oysters, conches, periwinkles, a few small turtles, and some other good fish."[35]

When food ran out, pirates often had to eat leather boots and satchels. One of Henry Morgan's half-starved buccaneers even left a recipe in 1670.

Slice the leather into pieces, then soak and beat and rub between stones to tenderise. Scrape off the hair, and roast or grill. Cut into smaller pieces and serve with lots of water.[36]

When real starvation set in, a few pirates turned to cannibalism. When food ran out on one ship, pirates killed and ate two African slaves.

Cool, Clear Water

If fresh food was scarce, freshwater was even harder to find. Salty ocean water is undrinkable, and hauling freshwater from inland streams required a huge amount of work. First, empty barrels had to be rowed ashore in a small boat. A fresh spring or stream had to be located and the barrels filled. Then, weighing several hundred pounds each, the water barrels had to be rolled back to the boat, rowed out to the ship, and hoisted on board.

John Esquemeling tells of the hardships of this task during foul weather:

I went with ten more of our company and two canoes, to fetch water from the land. Having filled our jars, we could not get back to the ship by reason of a Southerly wind that blew from off the ocean and hindered our return. Thus we were forced to lie still in a water-hole, and wait until the winds were over for a safe opportunity. [At night] we ventured out both canoes together but the winds were so high that we were forced to throw all our jars of water overboard to lighten our boats—otherwise we would have inevitably perished.[37]

In the meantime, Esquemeling's pirate ship had to leave the harbor so it would not get blown onshore by the winds. The men were stranded for days, but they finally found the ship after walking across the island. They returned to the mother ship without water, which then had to be collected all over again.

Water quickly grew stale when stored in rotting old barrels belowdecks. This is one reason that pirates preferred rum, wine, and beer to water.

Fun and Games

Pirates loved gambling and games as much as they loved their rum. Backgammon was a favorite of officers, but card games and dice were most popular among the average pirates. Gambling was such a serious problem that pirates sometimes lost everything they owned, even their clothing. And drinking and gambling often led to violence.

Esquemeling notes how one band of pirates shared 260,000 pieces of eight, but squandered it within three weeks, "having spent it all in things of little value, or at play

Ghosts and Haunted Ships

Pirates came from many religious backgrounds, including Catholic, Protestant, Muslim, and African religions. But when it came to the uncertainties of the sea with death lurking over every wave, pirates were quite a superstitious bunch. As long as there have been ships and shipwrecks, sailors have told ghost stories and tall tales about living wraiths from beneath the waves. Pirates were no different in this respect.

Surprisingly enough, most pirates feared the sea so much they never learned to swim. They thought it was better to drown quickly if they fell in, rather than float for hours and then die. And pirates believed that if the ocean was cheated of one life, it would soon seek another.

Superstitions influenced everything from the construction of the ship to the way pirates dressed. A ship built from oak was thought to protect it against lightning. Holly was thought to ward off evil. Falling stars meant good luck. The wooden bust of a woman placed on the stern of a ship was also believed to offer protection.

Pirates believed gold earrings helped keep a ship afloat. Iron horseshoes were a symbol of good luck. Brooms nailed to the mast were thought to sweep in good winds, but if a sailor whistled, it would bring up winds too strong. Above all, no dead man was to be kept on a ship. It was believed that if the dead were near, the sea would attack. If the dead man had been murdered or had died in battle, his ghost might drift about for centuries, tormenting all who gazed upon it.

---

of either cards or dice."[38] These sorts of losses led to the "no game at cards or dice for money" provisions in the pirate's code of conduct.

Storms and Shipwrecks

Pirates desperately feared capture by authorities. But relentless storms and hurricanes were a more constant threat. The Caribbean and the Gulf of Mexico are famous for their warm climate and sunny winters. But those same areas were (and still are) subject to fierce hurricanes that build up in the Atlantic and sweep across the islands in the region. In the days before forecasting equipment or radios, pirates never knew a hurricane was coming until it was too

late. And even if they were forewarned, there was little they could do about it.

The islands of the Caribbean are regular targets for ferocious storms. In 1712, a hurricane destroyed forty-seven ships in Jamaican harbors. On August 28, 1722, Port Royal was swamped by a hurricane. The sea threw up rocks and stones and sunk the town under five feet of water. Pirate Edward Low was caught in that hurricane. His crew was forced to jettison all their food, water, guns, and other heavy items overboard to lighten the ship.

Since pirates operated alone and left few records, no one knows how many ships were sunk by storms and hurricanes. But the unforgiving dangers of the sea killed many a pirate and took many a ship.

Into Action on the High Seas

Pirates lived to plunder, loot, and steal. Stolen booty was the payoff that justified all the hardships of life at sea. There was a certain method to the madness of pirate attacks that was developed over time. Like other aspects of pirate life, attacks were carried out in different ways at different times. But during piracy's golden age, pirates had refined their methods to the point that many offensives had similar characteristics. When there was a fight, it usually involved stealth, trickery, and surprise. With only two thousand or so pirates operating at any one time, the fine art of freebooting was a lesson pirates learned from one another.

Sizing Up the Victim

Pirates tried hard to build a reputation of great cruelty. Terror, or the threat of terror, was their most effective weapon. Since they were not fighting for king or country, most pirates did what they could to avoid out-and-out battle. They wanted to live long enough to enjoy their booty.

Lurking among the cays and islets of the Caribbean, pirates usually spotted their victims before they themselves were seen. In the open ocean, a lookout could see twenty miles when perched atop a one-hundred-foot mast. Once a ship was spotted, it was examined in detail to see what kind of vessel it was, what country it was from, where it was coming from, and what it might be carrying. Most important, pirates had to decide what sort of resistance a ship's crew would offer.

The buccaneer captain and crew would weigh the options and vote whether or not to attack. Since it was not always easy to tell how heavily armed a ship might be, the pirates might follow it for several hours, or even days. If the ship appeared too large or well armed, the pirates could simply veer away and wait for another, weaker ship.

Sometimes pirates snuck up on their victims by taking down the Jolly Roger and hoisting up the colors of a friendly nation. Pirates had no qualms about flying Dutch, English, Irish, or French flags, sometimes right above the Jolly Roger. But in general, pirates were so bold that they did not even bother to hide their black flag. When the skull and crossbones drew near, a ship's captain had plenty of time to think about surrender.

The Attack!

Once the pirates decided to attack, it could take several hours to come close to the merchantman. But a pirate sloop was faster than the merchantman, and escape was usually impossible unless the defenders could put up a fight and damage the pirate vessel. If the cargo ship offered no resistance, the pirate ship would pull alongside its victim. As the pirates drew close, the pirate band would produce horrendous noise. The pirates "vapored," as they called it, dancing around the poop deck, growling, chanting war cries, firing their pistols in the air, and waving cutlasses.

Often the merchant captain was singled out for abuse. Pirate captain John Russell hailed Captain George Roberts in this manner: "You dog! You son of a dog! You speckle-shirted dog! I will drub you, you dog, within an inch of your life—and that inch too!" Other pirates tried a friendlier approach. In 1697 pirate Robert Culliford hailed a cargo-rich ship by saying, "Gentlemen, we want not your ship, but only your money. Money we want and money we shall have."[39]

When the ships got close enough, the pirates usually ordered the merchant captain to come to the pirate ship. Longboats were hoisted over the side and the captain was ferried into the pirates' clutches. While the captain was held hostage, the pirates would swarm aboard their prey. They would tear open hatches and cargo with their boarding axes. They would cut open bales, trunks, and boxes with cutlasses. Cargo they deemed worthless was hacked apart and thrown overboard. Prizes were stacked up to be transported back to the pirate ship. Guns, riggings, rope, and sails were confiscated. Barrels of gunpowder, liquor, food, and water were loaded into longboats for transportation. As Captain Charles Johnson noted, this was usually done with "incessant cursing and swearing, more like fiends than men."[40]

Sea rogues pursue a treasure-laden merchantman. Such chases could last for hours, but often ships succumbed to the pirate attackers without resistance.

Pirates viciously hurl glass bottles at a sea captain who was held hostage during a raid.

When the plundering was over, the pirates turned their attention to the crew. Sometimes every person aboard the merchantman was forced, at gunpoint, to leave the ship and join the pirates. Other times only the surgeon, carpenter, or other sea artists were kidnapped. Once in the clutches of the pirates, victims were often forced to sign a code of conduct or other paper pledging their allegiance to the pirates.

Multiple Ship Attacks

If the sight of one pirate ship was enough to scare a merchant captain, what would he think of three or four ships? There are many examples of great pirate captains attacking with a squadron of ships. Bartholomew Roberts commanded four vessels at the height of his career in 1721. His flagship, the *Royal Fortune*, carried forty-two guns. The *Sea King* was a brigantine with thirty guns, as was the French-built ship *Ranger*. Roberts also had a small ship of sixteen guns that was used for storage. The total number of pirates under his command was 508.

Blackbeard operated three and sometimes four ships. Charles Vane commanded two. Sometimes pirate captains even teamed up and cruised together.

Axes, Cutlasses, and Daggers

When pirates attacked, they had the strength of their numbers to insure victory. But it did not hurt that each man was usually well armed with a cutlass, a pistol, and perhaps a dagger clenched between his teeth. The fear generated by a rush of sword-waving pirates was usually enough to force the immediate surrender of a merchant ship. Full-scale bloody attacks were the exception rather than the rule. If a merchant ship was caught by a pirate, the captain knew that, for the sake of his crew, it was better to hand over his cargo. If the captain did not give in, pirates had many weapons of persuasion in their arsenals.

The buccaneer attack upon the *Princess Galley* gives a clear picture of the manner in which pirates operated. The merchant ship *Princess Galley* was near the end of its voyage from Africa, coming into the southern region of the Caribbean on September 14, 1723. As it approached Barbados with a human cargo of slaves, the crew was alarmed to see the black flag on an approaching ship. As the ship drew closer, sailors on the *Princess Galley* could see it was a sloop with eight guns, ten swivel guns, and forty pirates.

The *Princess Galley*'s captain, John Wickstead, realized that his ship was no match for the pirates. After his feeble attempt to escape, the pirate ship began firing its guns. The heavily laden merchant ship was soon overtaken by George Lowther and his buccaneer crew. Captain Wickstead was ordered to send a boat across. A longboat was sent to the pirate ship, and several buccaneers jumped aboard and ferried back to the *Princess Galley*.

For the next twenty-four hours, the pirates held down Wickstead, the ship's surgeon, and the second mate. Lighted fuses were put between their fingers until they revealed the location of the gold on board. The pirates confiscated fifty-four ounces of gold and ransacked the ship. They took gunpowder, pistols, ropes, sails, and riggings. The pirates removed the merchant ship's cannons and swivel guns. Eleven slaves were brought up from the hold and ferried back to the pirates' ship.

Two seamen—the surgeon's mate and the carpenter's mate—were forced to join the pirates. Two other members of the crew voluntarily joined the pirates. Having stripped the *Princess Galley*, the pirates sailed away. Wickstead was left to make his way to Barbados.

This attack was typical of dozens of pirate missions in the early eighteenth century: The pirates sailed under the Jolly Roger with no attempt to disguise themselves; the victims offered no resistance; the pirates demanded the merchant captain send a boat across for them; the pirates took their time looting the ship.

When pirates scurried onto a ship, they pulled themselves up the side of the ship with a weapon called a boarding ax. The boarding ax was swung into the steep hull of the ship, and its sharp hatchet blade backed by a pointed end allowed a pirate to clamor aboard. Once on deck, the sharp blade could bring down the sails and netting with one swing, cutting through ropes as thick as a man's arm. Boarding axes also made brutal weapons in hand-to-hand combat.

Cutlasses had short, broad blades with leather-wrapped, bone, or ivory handles. They were ideal for fighting in hand-to-hand combat on the tight quarters of a ship, where a long sword could get tangled in the rigging.

According to legend, the cutlass was invented by the original buccaneers. The long knives used to butcher meat evolved into the short sword used by most pirates.

Daggers and dirks were small and efficient knives that pirates could conceal beneath their clothing. They were especially handy belowdecks where there was little space to swing a cutlass.

Hand Grenades

When pirates first attacked, they could create confusion and panic among their victims by throwing *granado* shells onto the ship. *Gra-*

nados were an early form of hand grenades common in the 1700s. Because of their shape, they were called *granados*, which means pomegranates, by the Spanish. *Granados* were called powder flasks by the English.

Granados were hollow balls made of iron or wood and filled with gunpowder. They weighed two ounces each and were lit by means of a fuse. When thrown aboard a ship, *granados* caused death and injury, giving the victims a quick reason to surrender.

Pistols and Muskets

The guns available to pirates were not as effective as modern arms. Muskets and flintlock pistols required several minutes to reload after firing. For this reason, some pirates—such as Blackbeard—carried as many as six pistols strapped across their chest.

Flintlocks needed to be packed with a bullet and gunpowder, which was rammed down the pistol's barrel with a long rod. The gunpowder was ignited by a spark of flint held on the gun's cock. Flintlocks were unreliable because the damp sea air made the powder wet, causing only a "flash in the pan." They took so long to reload that after a flintlock was fired, pirates simply used the butt end as a club.

The muskatoon, or blunderbuss, was a short-barreled rifle that fired a spray of lead pellets like a shotgun. It had limited accuracy and was used only at close range. Fired from the shoulder, the short barrel of the muskatoon was easier to handle on a ship's cramped deck than other guns.

The musket was a long-barreled rifle that offered accuracy from a distance. To keep the musket ball from rolling out of the gun barrel, the ball was wrapped in a cotton cloth to make it fit tight in the barrel. The rifle had spiral grooving in the barrel, which spun the musket ball so that it flew in a straight line. Muskets were accurate but difficult to aim from the deck of a heaving ship.

Cannons and Shot

If a merchantman did not surrender but instead tried to flee from its pursuers, then the pirates needed to incapacitate their prey with cannon fire. Pirate ships needed large crews to man their cannons. Each gun required a team of four to six men to load, aim, fire, and haul the cannon back into position after recoil. It also took men to operate the smaller swivel guns and men to work the ship. If a brigantine had twenty guns, it would take at

Wearing six pistols and carrying a cutlass, Blackbeard displayed an intimidating appearance.

Pirates menacingly wave their swords and fire a cannon to clear the decks of an enemy ship. Since long swords could become tangled in the ship's rigging, buccaneers used shorter cutlasses during hand-to-hand combat.

least forty to sixty men simply to operate all the cannons on one side of the ship.

A cannon could shoot a fifty-pound cannonball as far as one mile. Solid-shot cannonballs rarely sank a ship, but the impact of the iron balls created a tornado of deadly wooden splinters that devastated the crew. Cannonballs also took down masts and rigging, which left a ship unable to escape. Two cannonballs chained together were called chain shot; this variant was used to take down enemy sails and crew members. In addition to solid shot and chain shot, cannons might be loaded with buckshot, bar shot, nails, and spikes.

When all the cannons on one side of a ship were fired together it was called a broadside. Though rarely used—because the pirates did not want to damage what might be a prize ship—the broadside was a most fearful attack.

Stinkpots

Stinkpots were evil, foul-smelling grenades that pirates used to create confusion among their victims. In Pirates and Patriots of the Revolution, *C. Keith Wilbur describes a stinkpot.*

"A devilish concoction of salt peter (sodium nitrate), brimstone (sulfur), asafetida (malodorous gum resin of oriental plants of the carrot family) and decayed fish was packed into earthenware jugs. When the wick (called an ox-tail) was lit, the foul and suffocating mixture was hurled down from the main-tree and the nauseating smoke that spread through the hold and on deck could give an obstinate enemy second thoughts of resistance."

Kidnapping the Crew

Once a cargo ship was slowed or halted by cannon fire, the pirates could scramble aboard and freely ransack. Although items of resale value were of the utmost concern, pirates often began their looting by kidnapping useful crew members. The carpenter was the most important man on any ship—and the most likely to be kidnapped by pirates. The carpenter maintained all the wooden parts of a ship. He was constantly busy in heavy weather and was especially needed after a battle had shattered a vessel. On a pirate ship, with no access to shipyard repairs, the carpenter was even more crucial.

Another crew member who was often kidnapped was called the cooper. His job was to make barrels, an important job since every item of food and drink on a sailing ship—including dried beef, flour, biscuits, water, beer, wine, and spirits—was stored in barrels.

Kidnapped victims were always given the opportunity to willingly join the pirates, but stubborn merchant seamen were often compelled to go. This account comes from the *Boston Gazette* on November 29, 1725. It concerns a cooper named Ebenezer Mower.

One of the pirates struck Mower many blows on the head with the helve [handle] of an axe, whereby his head was much bruised and bloodied, after which the same pirate forced Mower to lay his head down on the hatch, and lifting the axe over his head swore that if he did not sign the Articles immediately, he would chop his head off. . . . Mower begged hard for his life.[41]

Sea artisans who were compelled to join ironically faced future jeopardy if they were caught as part of a pirate crew. If a pirate ship was captured by the navy, all men aboard were tried and punished as pirates, even if they were unwilling converts. When their names were signed on the articles, as Mower's was, they were guilty in the eyes of the law and punished by death.

Games of Torture

While pirates had a strict code of conduct among themselves, their victims were not so lucky. Pirates played with their prey like a cat with a mouse. They took a psychopathic delight in another's misery, and used torture and violence as sport.

English captain William Snelgrave was a prisoner of pirates for three weeks in 1719. He watched in horror as a French captain who did not surrender immediately was tortured. "They put a rope about his neck and hoisted him up and down several times to the Main-yard-arm, till he was almost dead."[42]

A pirate crew works together to load and fire a mighty cannon during the heat of battle. Although these guns rarely sank an enemy vessel, their deadly shot could cause massive injury to a crew and immobilize a ship.

A pirate hangs from the yardarm of a ship. Tortures such as this were usually reserved for prisoners, not the pirates themselves.

Other pirate torments included a vicious game called *sweating*, where a victim was forced to run around the mizzenmast (middle mast of a three-masted ship) while he was jabbed by pitchforks. This game ended when the victim dropped. Some victims were tied to the mizzenmast and used as a target for pistol practice.

John Esquemeling describes some of the pirate tortures he witnessed during the seventeenth century:

Among other tortures then used, one was to stretch their limbs with cords, and at the same time beat them with sticks and other instruments. Others had burning matches placed betwixt their fingers, which were thus burnt alive. Others had slender chords twisted about their heads, till their eyes had burst out of the skull.[43]

Other tortures are almost too horrible to recount. Victims were burnt alive, had stone piled upon them, or had their intestines pulled out slowly.

As author Peter Newark explains, when the schooner *Mary* was attacked by pirates in the Strait of Florida, terrible savagery occurred.

They tied a passenger to the mainmast, and hanged one of the crew from the foreyard, and nailed the bosun to the deck, driving spikes through his feet and arms. The rest of the crew, except the captain, were bound and blindfolded and placed in front of a swivel gun and blown to bits. The captain, who refused to divulge the hiding place of a large sum of money, was subjected to a most fiendish death; they hacked off both his arms and burnt him alive on a bed of tarred oakum.[44]

Treating Wounds

Many pirates were wounded in battle by the same type of weapons they used on their victims. Primitive medicine usually allowed no more treatment than the sawing off of a limb. Author Peter Newark describes pirate surgery.

"Pirates wounded in battle were lucky to survive the primitive surgery. There were, of course, no anesthetics (a bottle of rum would have to suffice) and even if they lived through the ordeal of saw and knife, gangrene and other infections would finish them off. The stumps of amputated limbs were cauterized with boiling tar or pitch. The same conditions [existed] on naval vessels."

African slaves huddle together in the crowded quarters of a slave ship. The slave trade flourished during the seventeenth and eighteenth centuries.

The catalog of pirate cruelties is almost endless. And the pirate ship had an endless supply of instruments for torture. There were boat hooks, hammers, and iron bars for beatings; ropes of all sizes for whipping, strangling, and stretching; and barrels of salt to pour into wounds.

Pirates learned much of their cruelty in the navy, which commonly used whippings, burnings, hangings, and other torture and violence upon its own men. The government courts were not much better. In fact, punishments meted out by English courts were often as barbaric as any dreamed up by pirates. One motive for pirate violence was revenge against sailors of nations that had tortured and hanged pirates.

While some pirates were notoriously cruel, many only resorted to torture if they had to. A small amount of violence usually caused crew and passengers to quickly give over their valuables. In nine out of ten pirate attacks, the victims gave up quickly, the pirates stole what they wanted, and no one was hurt. But, like today, stories of violence and torture sold books and newspapers, and so a good record was left behind of pirate cruelties.

Pirates and Slavery

Pirates practiced a code of justice among themselves. But it did not usually extend to black Africans. When pirates captured a merchant ship, they often found a cargo of half-dead slaves, chained beneath decks. The slave trade was a huge business in the seventeenth and eighteenth centuries, and slaves sold in America brought ten to fifteen times the price of their cost in Africa. Slaves had absolutely no human rights and were treated as if they were any other product. Huge profits lured many pirates into the slave trade. It was so common in fact that the term *picaroon* was coined to describe a pirate slave trader. One notable picaroon was John Hawkins, who loaded three hundred slaves in his ship in Africa and sold them in Hispaniola on his first Caribbean voyage.

Booty, Trash, and Treasure

Unless revenge was the motive—or a captain would not hand over the goods—pirates were usually more concerned with looting than with physical violence. The longer a pirate remained on a victim's ship, the better the odds of something going wrong. The buccaneers' preferred method was to strike, steal, and sail away.

Much of the loot pirates carried off has been termed *household goods*. These items consisted of food, drink, ropes, and sails. When pirates knocked over the *Restoration* in 1717, they carried off "sails, pump-bolts, log-lines, needles, twine, kettle, [and] frying pans." The sloop *Content* was overrun near Barbados, with pirates stealing "fourteen boxes of candles, two boxes of soap, together with a flying-jib, flying-jib-boom, flying-jib-halliards, main halliards, anchor and cable and several carpenters tools."[45]

Calico Jack Rackam went on a two-year cruise in the West Indies and raided more

Calico Jack Rackam raided more than twenty ships during a two-year spree.

than twenty ships. But most were small fishing boats and small traders. On one schooner, Jack reported that all he was able to steal was "50 rolls of tobacco and nine bags of pimento."[46]

After months at sea, pirates were often in desperate need of medical supplies. In 1720 Edward England plundered the ship *Cassandra*. He and his crew stole goods worth tens of thousands of dollars. But as one of the victims reported, "No part of a ship's cargo was as valued by the robbers as much as the doctor's chest, for all were poxed to a great degree."[47]

Most pirate booty was only valuable if the buccaneers could sell or trade it. That is why silver and gold coins were a favorite treasure. They could be easily divided among the crew or spent in towns and cities. Jewels were hard to divide and had to be sold, often below market value.

The Riches of Piracy

The pirates who managed to rack up huge scores of loot were men whose names are still mentioned today. They captured the imaginations of people in the seventeenth and eighteenth centuries, and their deeds were subject to countless articles, books, plays, and movies in the centuries following.

In 1717 Sam Bellamy was cruising between Cuba and Hispaniola when the slave ship *Whydah* came into sight. Bellamy chased the ship for three days, finally catching up with it near the Bahamas. *Whydah* offered little resistance and the pirates soon swarmed aboard. The buccaneers were overjoyed as they found the ship to contain ivory, indigo, sugar, quinine (a cure for malaria), gold, and silver. Bellamy seized the entire vessel, leaving his old ship behind. Like many other pirates, Bellamy's luck soon deserted him. A few weeks later, the *Whydah* was caught in a gale near Cape Cod.

The ship broke apart on a shoal, and 144 men, including Bellamy, drowned.

Black Bart, though never as famous as other pirates, was one of the most successful—and most brazen. At one point in his career he attacked several in a fleet of forty-two Portuguese merchant ships. While dozens of the merchant captains looked on, Bart made off with ninety thousand gold coins, a cross inlaid with diamonds that was bound for the king of Portugal, chains and jewels, and a cargo of sugar, skins, and tobacco.

Captain Kidd's Buried Treasure

Like many other aspects of pirate stories, tales of buried treasure are often exaggerated or complete fiction. After months of misery at sea, when pirates returned home, they preferred to spend their stolen loot on wine, women, and song, or gamble it away. Though there were several cases of pirates burying trunks of gold and silver, it was only when the buccaneers were being pursued by authorities. Once the pressure was off, the treasure was quickly recovered.

The pirate who was most responsible for tales of buried treasure is also the most well known: Captain Kidd. It is odd that the name of William Kidd has been linked with piracy. He never thought of himself as a pirate and maintained his innocence until the bitter end. But rumors were spread that Kidd buried plundered silver and gold on Gardiners Island near New York before he was arrested. This rumor persisted for centuries and made the name Captain Kidd synonymous with buried treasure.

Captain Kidd was a successful businessman and an ex-privateer. He was talked into joining a pirate-hunting expedition in the Indian Ocean, where John Avery was disrupting trade. Investors in the scheme would split the

Successful pirate Black Bart boldly wears the diamond-inlaid cross stolen from a ship belonging to the king of Portugal.

valuables Kidd was supposed to bring back from Avery.

Kidd's expedition was full of misfortune. Half his crew was lost to a navy press gang. So in 1696, Kidd's ship the *Adventure Galley* set sail from New York with a crew of "men of desperate fortunes and necessities, thirsty for treasure and with few scruples about how they obtained it."[48]

As the cruise progressed, Kidd became increasingly aggressive and unable to control his crew. He began attacking nonpirate vessels with the violence he was to have saved for John Avery. Yet he still maintained he was working within the law. In October 1697, Kidd killed a crew member after an argument. The crew threatened mutiny.

In January 1698, Captain Kidd seized the *Quedah Merchant*, taking its cargo of silk, calico, sugar, opium, and iron. The ship was flying French flags, and Kidd had a letter of marque to attack French ships. But the ship was actually owned by Armenians. This was proven by the *Quedah Merchant*'s captain, but Kidd proceeded anyway. With this act William Kidd crossed the line—becoming an ordinary pirate instead of a privateer. Upon reaching port, he sold the *Quedah Merchant*'s cargo. As soon as Kidd divided up the money among his crew, most of them jumped ship, leaving Kidd with eighteen men to return to New York. On the way back, Kidd looted several more ships. While in the Caribbean he learned that the British government had declared him a pirate.

Mysterious Trips to Gardiners Island

After three years at sea, Kidd made a desperately difficult journey back to America. He thought that he could justify his acts under the guise of privateering, but authorities accused him of piracy. Captain Kidd tried to negotiate his freedom, with no success. During the course of the next several weeks, he sailed his ship back and forth between New York City and Gardiners Island on the eastern tip of Long Island. Kidd left five bales of cloth, a chest of fine goods, and fifty-two pounds of gold with his friend—and the island's owner—John Gardiner.

Kidd was soon locked up in Boston's jail. Authorities tried to locate some of the stolen booty, which was scattered about in New York, Boston, and the West Indies. Some of the treasure was recovered. John Gardiner turned in eleven bags of gold and silver. But the full amount of Kidd's take was never found. Over the years, people have searched Gardiners Island looking for Captain Kidd's buried treasure. But the searches turned up nothing.

Captain Kidd was sent back to England for a trial. He was found guilty of murder and five

Pirates bury their ill-gotten treasure in a scene from The Pirate's Own Book. *Buccaneers rarely buried their booty; most spent the loot as soon as it was acquired.*

Captain Kidd attempts to quell a mutiny by swinging a bucket at a disobedient crew member. Although Kidd continued to maintain that he was a legal privateer, his exploits identified him as a lawless pirate.

counts of piracy. On May 23, 1701, Kidd, who was allowed to get extremely drunk, was strung up on the gallows. But when he was hanged, the rope broke, dropping him into the mud. The second time the noose held. His body was then covered with tar, bound with iron bands, and left to hang by the Thames River. His grisly, rotting corpse dangled there for several years as "a greater Terrour to all Persons from committing ye like Crimes for the time to come."[49]

Exotic Ports of Call

Pirates, freebooters, and buccaneers spent a great amount of their time on land partying and planning their next mission. Trips ashore allowed pirates to get off of their pitching, stinking ships, sell their stolen booty, and enjoy the fruits of their labors in local taverns. Some pirates, fresh from a profitable raid, took their money and invested in plantations and businesses. Others snuck back to their homes in England, France, or Spain. But most wasted their money in a few weeks and were soon back on the high seas looking for more loot.

Favorite Pirate Haunts

Buccaneers lived in dozens of towns and villages in the Americas. But their favorite haunts were the islands of Jamaica, Hispaniola, and the tiny isle of Tortuga. The pirates were easily spotted among the more law-abiding citizens of the Caribbean. They were often seen rampaging up and down the streets, blind drunk, at all hours of the day and night. They threw away their money quickly. As Esquemeling noted, the pirates

> wasted in a few days in the taverns and stews all they had gotten, by giving themselves to all manner of debauchery with strumpets [prostitutes] and wine. Such of these pirates are found who will spend 2 or 3 thousand pieces of eight in one night, not leaving themselves a good shirt to

wear on their backs in the morning. Thus upon a certain time I saw one of them give unto a common strumpet 500 pieces of eight only that he might see her naked.[50]

Pirates also did on land what they did so well at sea—plunder, steal, and murder. Towns large and small were easy pickings for bands of bloodthirsty pirates. They stole from Native Americans, housewives, and soldiers behind high fort walls. No place was safe, and

Black Bart's crew carouses on the shores of the Calabar River in Africa.

some towns were trounced again and again—even if they were located far inland where sea robbers would not be expected.

Tortuga's Buccaneer Brethren

In 1630 the Spanish succeeded in driving the original buccaneers from Hispaniola. The *boucaniers* settled on a tiny, turtle-shaped island on the north side of Hispaniola. Called Tortuga, the isle is about twenty-five miles long and three miles wide. It was named by Columbus for the great sea turtle, *tortuga de mar* in Spanish. Tortuga offered the buccaneers freshwater, fertile land, good anchorages, and a defensible harbor. And it lay on the Windward Passage, a sea current frequented by trade ships between Cuba and Hispaniola.

Later, when the Spanish forced English and French colonists from St. Kitts and Hispaniola, they also went to Tortuga, which quickly became "the common place of refuge of all sorts of wickedness, the seminary of pirates and thieves."[51]

One of the first buccaneer leaders on Tortuga was a Frenchman named Jean le Vasseur, who had once been a military engineer. Le Vasseur built a fort on a rocky hill above the harbor, named it Fort de Rocher, and armed it with twenty-four guns. Buccaneers in le Vasseur's fort repelled several Spanish attempts to take back the island.

John Esquemeling wrote much of his book *The Buccaneers of America* about the wicked pirates of Tortuga. There was Roche Brasiliano who

> many times being in drink, he would run up and down the streets, beating and wounding [all] whom he met, no person daring to oppose him.

Francis L'Olonnais, the dreaded slave turned boucanier, *terrorized the citizens of Tortuga.*

Unto the Spaniards he always showed himself very barbarous and cruel. He commanded several [Spaniards] to be roasted alive upon wooden spits, for no other crime than they would not show him the places, or hog-yards, where he might steal swine.[52]

Another ne'er-do-well who terrorized Tortuga was Francis L'Olonnais. Originally brought to Hispaniola as a French slave, L'Olonnais was an original *boucanier* whose acts of cruelty made him famous. According to Esquemeling,

> It was the custom of L'Olonnais that, having tormented any persons and they not confessing, he would instantly cut them to pieces with his hanger [cutlass], first some flesh, then a hand, an arm, a leg . . . and then pull out their tongue.[53]

Island Medicines

The islands of the Caribbean were rich in wild foods, herbal medicines, and other resources valued by pirates. John Esquemeling wrote in The Buccaneers of America *about the helpful plants on the isle of Tortuga.*

"As to the wood that grows on the island, the trees are exceedingly tall and pleasing to the sight; whence no man will doubt but they may be applied to several uses with great benefit. Such is the Yellow Saunder, which tree by the inhabitants of this country is called English Candlewood, because it burns like a candle, and serves them with light while they use their fishery in the night. Here also grows . . . *guaiacum*, the virtues of which are very well known, physicians drawing from hence, the greatest antidote for all venereal diseases, and also for cold and vicious humors.

The island is not deficient in aloes, or an infinite number of other medicinal herbs, which may please the curiosity of such as are given to their contemplation. Moreover for the building of ships, or any other sort of architecture, here are found, in this spot of Neptune, several sorts of timber very convenient. There fruits, likewise, which here abundantly grow, are nothing inferiour, as to their quantity or quality. I shall name only some of the most ordinary and common. Such are magniot [manioc root for flour], potatoes, acajou apples [cashew nuts], yannas [yams], bacones, paquayes, carosoles, mamayn, ananas [pineapples], and diverse other sorts, which, not to be tedious, I omit. Here also grows those trees called palmettos whence is drawn a certain juice which serves inhabitants instead of wine, and whose leaves do cover their houses instead of tiles."

The evil buccaneer once ripped open a man's chest with his cutlass and began gnawing on his still-beating heart. L'Olonnais met a fitting end. After stealing millions of dollars worth of gold from the Spanish, he was captured by Native Americans who cut him into pieces, which they burned, casting the ashes to the winds to ensure he would never return.

Characters like L'Olonnais roamed Tortuga for about twenty-five years. But Spanish, and then French, raids on the tiny island eventually drove the pirates to other places. Foremost among those places was Port Royal, Jamaica.

The Wicked Town of Port Royal

In 1655 England gained control of Jamaica, which lay in the very heart of the Spanish Caribbean. English buccaneers who had been driven off of other islands found an ideal base on this sparsely populated island. Port Royal was situated on a narrow spit of land on the southern side of Jamaica. Today it is a tiny fishing village. But for twenty years, from 1672 to 1692, Port Royal was one of the richest and busiest ports in the Americas. And it was home to the largest concentration of pirates in the Caribbean.

In its boomtown days, Port Royal was home to almost eight thousand people, including carpenters, goldsmiths, sail makers, shipwrights, and seamen. It was also the largest slave port in the West Indies, where some twelve thousand black Africans were bought and sold between 1671 and 1679. The town looked like Bristol, England, with four-story brick and timber houses on streets with familiar English names like Thames Street, Queen Street, Smith's Alley, and Fisherman's Row.

Port Royal's wharves were lined with merchant ships and warehouses filled with tobacco, spices, sugar, beef, wine, and beer. The town had three churches, two prisons, and at least forty-four taverns. But it was the buccaneers who gave the town its reputation—and much of its wealth.

British governors actively encouraged piracy. The authorities believed that heavily armed pirate ships would repel French and Spanish attacks on Jamaica. It was a successful policy—no attacks were ever attempted. Meanwhile, Port Royal merchants became rich from plundered Spanish goods.

Onshore with a chest of booty, two pirates begin to fight over the treasure. Many freebooters brought their loot back to Port Royal, the infamous haven of cutthroat pirates.

Governors freely issued letters of marque to anyone who would harass the Spanish on ship or on land. So much plundered gold and silver flowed into Port Royal that the government proposed setting up a mint because proportionate to the population there was "more plenty of running cash than in London."[54]

With a harbor capable of sheltering five hundred ships, Port Royal was pirate paradise.

> The town rapidly filled with buccaneers and their loot: gold and silver in bullion and coins, Bars and cakes of gold, wedges and pigs of silver, Pistoles, Pieces of Eight and several other coins of both metals, with store wrought Plate, jewels, rich pearl necklaces, and of Pearl unsorted and drilled . . . bushels.[55]

The pirates' playground soon filled up with brothels, grog shops, and gaming houses. The free-spending freebooters drove off honest folk, including one clergyman who wrote, "Since the majority of its population consists of pirates, cutthroats, whores, and some of the vilest persons in the whole of the world, I felt my performance there was of no use."[56]

Brutal and frequent buccaneer raids drove Jamaican-based Spanish colonists into the hills. From 1655 to 1661, pirates based in Port Royal plundered eighteen cities, four towns, and thirty-six smaller settlements. Some villagers were brutalized over and over again, including those who lived far inland.

Judgment upon the Pirates' Port

The glory days of Port Royal ended at exactly 11:40 A.M. on July 7, 1692. At that moment, an incredibly violent earthquake hit the pirates' paradise. The unpaved streets rose and fell while brick and stone buildings collapsed. The earth opened up and swallowed entire houses. The wharf and two entire streets full of shops and houses next to the harbor dropped into the ocean. A tidal wave caused by the quake swept through the town. Two thousand people died in an instant and another two thousand died within weeks from wounds, diseases, and fever.

Some called it a judgment of God on an evil town. But the earthquake and following tremors did not deter

a company of lewd rogues whom they call privateers, [who] fell into breaking open warehouses and houses deserted, to rob

and rifle their neighbours whilst the earth trembled under them, and some of the houses fell on them in the act; and those audacious whores that remain still upon the place, are as impudent and as drunken as ever.[57]

Most of Port Royal disappeared that day: Two-thirds of the town simply sank beneath the waves. There were so few survivors that no one could clean up the dead bodies that drifted in the tide or lay on rocks and beaches.

Over the centuries Port Royal was partially rebuilt. Today the quiet village with the notorious past is a magnet to treasure hunters and archaeologists. Teams of divers occasion-

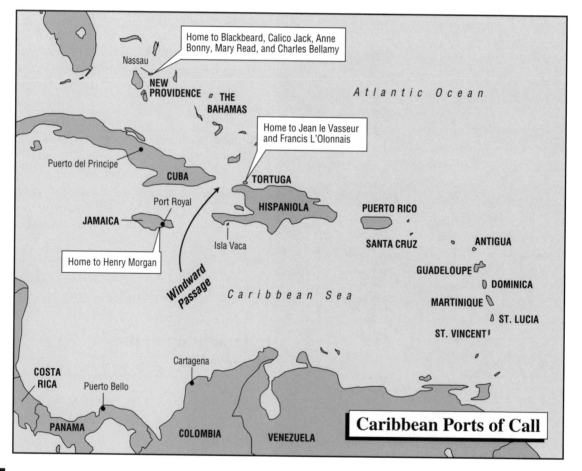

Caribbean Ports of Call

ally bring up interesting objects, including working silver watches and chests full of pieces of eight.

The King of the Buccaneers

One of the most famous buccaneers in Port Royal, and indeed the world, was a Welshman named Henry Morgan. Born in 1635, Morgan came to the Caribbean as a soldier. He was in the British forces that first captured Jamaica from the Spanish. Before long, Morgan had joined up with privateers who gleefully plundered Spanish towns in Central America. By the age of thirty-two, Morgan had established himself as a brilliant military leader. He was elected admiral of the Brethren of the Coast, the loose association of pirates and privateers who became known as buccaneers.

Henry Morgan organized the world's largest pirate expeditions. And they were also wildly successful. In 1668, operating from a base in Port Royal, Morgan led seven hundred fighting buccaneers in twelve ships to a raid on the city of Puerto del Principe (now Camagüey), Cuba.

The town's men, women, and children were rounded up and locked in several churches. The pirates pillaged for several days, feasting and drinking, while the poor townspeople starved. Morgan demanded five hundred head of cattle be butchered and salted by the prisoners and then delivered to his ships or he would burn the town to the ground. After the Spaniards did his bidding, Morgan and the pirates sailed back to Port Royal.

Plundering Puerto Bello

Later the same year, Morgan led a band of buccaneers to an attack on Puerto Bello—the third largest city in the New World—on the

Welsh pirate Henry Morgan dominated the pirate scene in Port Royal.

Henry Morgan and his buc-caneers extort tribute from the citizens of Panama.

eastern coast of Panama. Puerto Bello was a treasure port where the Spaniards loaded their ships full of gold and silver bound for Spain. Being such an important town, Puerto Bello was heavily fortified with two castles overlooking the bay. Morgan's only hope of taking the town was through complete surprise.

Morgan sailed from Port Royal with 460 men and landed 100 miles up the coast from Puerto Bello. The buccaneers transferred to twenty-three canoes and approached the city around midnight. Before dawn on July 11, the pirates captured the lookout post. Shouting and screaming, the men charged one castle, where sleepy soldiers fired only one shot.

The pirates ran past the defensive position and into town. Once again, terrified men, women, and children were herded into churches. Pirate marksmen mounted a hill and picked off soldiers on the other castle's walls with their long-barreled muskets. By the time the sun rose fully in the sky, the 460 buccaneers found themselves in possession of Puerto Bello.

Using the mayor, old men, friars, and nuns as human shields, the buccaneers took over

Puerto Bello's castles. The red colors of the pirates were hoisted along with the English flag. Soldiers who resisted were shot. The rest of the day was spent looting and "lording it with wine and women."[58] Morgan's squadron of ships sailed into the harbor and dropped anchor. The buccaneers set off on a month-long spree of torture, rape, and murder.

Morgan sent a letter to the president of Panama demanding 350,000 pesos ransom or the city of Puerto Bello would be burned to the ground. The president refused and sent eight hundred soldiers. But torrential rains and a shortage of food demoralized the Spaniards. After three weeks, a mule train was sent to Morgan containing about 90,000 pesos in gold and silver. With the treasure looted from the town—usually taken by extreme torture—Morgan's booty amounted to 250,000 pesos.

Morgan set sail with his ransom and returned to Port Royal to a hero's welcome. For the next few weeks, the town was overwhelmed by drinking, gambling, and womanizing as the buccaneers squandered their money. The capture of Puerto Bello was the most successful amphibious attack of the seventeenth century.

Plans Exploded

Before long, the buccaneers had spent their money and began demanding that Morgan set out on another mission. In early 1669, Morgan began plotting to take Isla Vaca, one of the Spanish treasure ports off the coast of Hispaniola. Ten ships and eight hundred men gathered for the heist. Morgan held a war council on his ship. After a rowdy dinner aboard the ship, some drunken gunners set off their muskets. A spark ignited a powder barrel, which exploded, blowing up the ship

and killing several hundred men, including those across the table from Morgan.

As the sea turned red with blood, Morgan walked away from the conflagration unharmed. Buccaneers from the other ships quickly rowed to the scene and stripped the dead of their valuables, even hacking off fingers to get gold rings. The loss of some two hundred men put an end to the plans to raid Isla Vaca.

The Attack of Panama

In late 1670, Morgan raised a fleet of forty ships and two thousand men to capture Panama City, a place called "the golden warehouse of the Indies." This was Morgan's largest expedition—and his most difficult. Panama is a small country on the isthmus of Central America. One side of the country faces the Caribbean on the east and the other side faces the Pacific on the west. Panama City would have to be reached overland and taken by surprise from the east.

On December 19, 1670, the largest buccaneer fleet ever assembled sailed to Fort San Lorenzo on the east coast of Panama. After several days of fierce fighting, the English flag flew above the fort. Morgan's fleet sailed past the silenced guns and headed up the Chagres River. A few miles up the river they transferred to small boats and canoes. After several more miles, fourteen hundred pirates set out on foot to Panama City.

The pirates had no food and found very little in the villages along the way. They marched for seven days through the hot jungle. Weakened by hunger, dysentery, and fever, the buccaneers were ambushed several times by hostile Spaniards. Some men resorted to eating their boiled shoes and satchels. When the treasure hunters finally sighted Panama City, they saw the billowing sails of great galleons sailing *away* from the city with millions of dollars worth of gold, silver, and jewels. Though the treasure eluded them, the band did slaughter some cattle and finally get to eat.

When the pirates marched on the city, they found twenty-seven hundred Spanish soldiers in battle formation. Morgan pretended to retreat, so the Spanish surged forward. The buccaneers, facing a disorganized group of men and horses, stood their ground and fired. The leading horsemen were brought down by French marksmen, and the rest turned and ran. The soldiers on foot were easy prey for the sharpshooting buccaneers. By midmorning five hundred Spanish soldiers lay dead or wounded under the tropical sun, with only fifteen pirates killed in battle.

Rather than have Panama fall into enemy hands, the retreating Spaniards destroyed it. Principal buildings were set on fire and powder barrels were detonated. The fort was blown up so hastily that forty soldiers were still inside when it exploded. Citizens fled to the woods. By the time the buccaneers marched into the city and extinguished the flames, three-quarters of Panama was leveled. Gone were more than two hundred richly stocked warehouses and the homes of the richest citizens. "Thus was consumed the famous and ancient city of Panama, the greatest mart for silver and gold in the whole world,"[59] Morgan later wrote.

Morgan's Panama Loot

The buccaneers spent a month in the burned-out city. They hunted down Spaniards and tortured them to find out where riches had been stashed. The greatest prize of all was overlooked by the pirates: The great altar of the cathedral was made from

gold. A friar had hastily painted it with whitewash, and the pirates never noticed.

Most of Morgan's loot came from ransoming prisoners. It included 750,000 pieces of eight, gold doubloons, silver bars, ingots, pearls, jewelry, silks, and spices. It took 175 mules to carry it across the isthmus.

As would be expected, when the loot was divided up, there was rebellion among the pirates. Morgan claimed the lion's share for himself. The other men received only two hundred pieces of eight each. This seemed far too little after weeks of starving and fighting. Morgan did not want to hear about it. He and the crew of his ship lifted anchor and sailed off without waiting to hear the complaints of his dissatisfied allies. The remaining pirates set off in different directions. The French contingent, about one-third of the men, went back to Tortuga. Many headed north to Honduras, while some followed Morgan back to Jamaica. The sack of Panama was the last major mission of the buccaneers. Piracy continued and increased, but nothing on the scale of Morgan's actions was ever seen again.

Morgan returned to Jamaica as a hero. But the news of Panama's destruction was not well received in Spain, or in England. England was at peace with Spain during this time, and the queen of Spain was "in such a distemper and excess of weeping and violent passion as those about her feared it might shorten her life."[60]

In April 1672, to appease Spain, Henry Morgan was arrested by British authorities and sent back to England. He had been ill with fever for several months and there was much sympathy for his condition. Morgan was never imprisoned and waited in London for two years to hear his fate. Instead of arrest, Morgan was appointed assistant to the lieutenant governor of Jamaica and given knighthood by King Charles II. Sir Henry

Morgan returned to Jamaica in 1676. He built up Port Royal's fortifications and lived the life of a wealthy planter. But Morgan continued to gamble and drink. His alcoholism eventually killed him in 1688.

New Providence

After the Port Royal earthquake of 1692, pirates needed a new base of operations. For a short time, the island of Madagascar in the Indian Ocean served that purpose. But it was too far away from the riches of the New World.

In the early eighteenth century a pirate named Henry Jennings landed on the island of New Providence in the Caribbean. He figured this to be the perfect pirate haven in the region. The harbors were exactly the right depth—too shallow for British warships, but just deep enough for pirate schooners. The high hills of coral afforded a hawk's eye view of approaching prizes or enemies. The reef was laden with lobster, turtle, conch, and fish.

In the center of the island an abundance of huge trees towered over freshwater springs, wild boar, pigeons, and fruit.

Jennings dropped anchor in New Providence, and before long dozens of other pirates followed. By 1710 a community of freebooters, buccaneers, privateers, and other brigands was thriving. There were about five hundred law-abiding British families there, but they did not mind the pirates. They welcomed the money and goods the pirates brought to the island. Famed pirates based in New Providence included Blackbeard, Calico Jack, Mary Read, Anne Bonny, Charles Bellamy, and others.

The prized merchant ships and European traders crossing on the Windward Passage were a quick sail from New Providence. And when the pirates came home, they celebrated in the town of Nassau. Today, Nassau is the largest city on New Providence and the capital of the Bahamas. But in those days the town was really nothing but dozens of tents made from old sails pitched on the white-sand

Morgan Sues for Libel

It is not only in modern times that people sue publishers for printing questionable or harmful statements. When John Esquemeling's book *The Buccaneers of America* was first published in England, the publishers sent two copies to Henry Morgan. Morgan promptly sued. Esquemeling, who had been with Morgan on the raid of Panama, was bitterly disappointed when his take was only two hundred pieces of eight. Throughout the book, Esquemeling portrays Morgan as a cruel villain with no scruples.

Morgan sued for two hundred English pounds. He strongly objected to a passage that said he first went to the West Indies as an indentured servant. "I was never a servant to anyone in my life," Morgan thundered. "Unless to His Majesty." Morgan was also outraged at being called a pirate. Apparently Morgan had no objections to the portrayals of his torture and cruelties inflicted upon innocent citizens.

Later editions of *The Buccaneers of America* were changed, and Morgan was awarded £200 for damages by the king's court. Earlier versions of the book continued to circulate, however, and have been quoted to this day.

In 1717, King George I of England sent warships to New Providence in an attempt to rid the island of its pirate population.

beach. The only permanent buildings were taverns. There was no law in Nassau but fists, pistols, and cutlasses wielded by buccaneers.

The British authorities were seriously alarmed at this nest of pirates in their midst. On September 3, 1717, the king of England issued three measures to be taken against the pirates of New Providence. The first was to send three warships to the Caribbean. The second was to offer a pardon to any pirates who surrendered themselves. And the third was to appoint a governor of the Bahamas "who will be enabled to drive the pirates from the lodgment at Harbour Island and Providence."[61]

The king's proclamations were the beginning of the end for piracy in the Caribbean. Times were changing. England was becoming a world power, while Spain was fading from the scene. The British colonies in North America were generating a different sort of wealth—timber, cotton, tobacco, and natural resources. With a strong military presence in the Americas, the pirates would no longer have free reign to plunder at will. One by one the great pirate commanders would fall, and so too would the curtain on the golden age of piracy.

The Hunters Become the Hunted

The year 1717 was a high watermark for pirate activity. About two thousand pirates roamed the seas throughout America's thirteen colonies, the Caribbean, and South America. While their numbers seem small by today's standards, with eighty to one hundred pirates per ship, undermanned merchant ships had no chance.

Government officials complained bitterly. The governor of Bermuda said, "North and South Americas are infested with these rogues." The governor of Jamaica said, "There is hardly one ship or vessel coming in or going out of this island that is not plundered."[62] Trade was almost paralyzed. Ships could only leave Jamaica in convoy under naval escort. Merchants' insurance rates were astronomical.

Authorities in London were well aware of the piracy problem. But naval ships were chronically undermanned as a result of sickness, desertion, and death. And the navy men in the Caribbean had little interest in tangling with pirates—there was more profit in trading with them.

The Suppression of Pirates

By the end of the 1600s it became obvious that old English laws were not doing enough to stamp out piracy. Original antipirate laws from the 1500s stated that no English pirate could be hanged unless he confessed his crimes before a court. Confession of crimes was highly unlikely, and few freebooters were punished.

Early pirate laws were amended in 1536 by a decree that called for "the punishment of pirates and robbers of the sea." This later law stated that cases of piracy would be heard in a London court before England's lord high admiral and four judges. This new court proved itself efficient. More pirates were hanged in its first two years than in the previous two hundred. The problem was that Caribbean and colonial governors would have to capture pirates and ship them back to London for trial and punishment.

In 1700 the Act for the More Effectual Suppression of Piracy was passed in England. This ended the requirement that pirates be tried by the lord high admiral. It authorized the use of the death penalty anywhere on or near the sea. And it offered a percentage of the cargo to honest seamen who repelled pirate attacks.

The Execution Docks

Before 1700, most English pirates were imprisoned in the Tower of London or Newgate Prison after capture. If convicted, they met their end one mile away at the Execution Docks at Wapping, on the north bank of the Thames River. Wapping was populated by seamen, shipwrights, dock workers, and their families. The docks were a jumble of lumberyards, wharves, cranes, and warehouses. Ships were tied to the docks three and four deep.

A hanging at Wapping was an event that turned out the entire community. Vendors sold food and drink among the thick crowd that was busy smoking, drinking, and betting on the exact details of the pirate's impending death. Ships and boats moored in the river to watch the spectacle.

The condemned man traveled in a cart to the gallows, accompanied by a prison chaplain. Once he reached the riverside, the pirate was given the chance to speak to the crowd. Some muttered a few words of apology. Others spit and cursed and spoke defiantly, sometimes at great length.

A few rogues went to their death dressed in fine silk and velvet, throwing handfuls of gold coins and pearls on the way to the gallows. The crowd waited for the last words and applauded those who "died well." Those who did not were jeered.

Death by Hanging

The gallows were simply two uprights and a crossbeam. The pirate was marched up a ladder, the noose attached to the crossbeam was placed around his neck, and the ladder was jerked away. This did not always kill the pirate immediately. If he was left dangling, it was not unusual for a pirate's relatives to pull on his twitching legs to put him out of his agony. Sometimes the rope broke, dropping the pirate in the river muck, in which case, the muddy man was marched up the ladder to do it all over again.

Trials and Tribulations

Captured pirates had little chance to escape the noose. Publicity surrounded the trials, and pirate feats and foibles were exaggerated in handbills and newspapers. Pronouncements by judges, lawyers, and clergy left little doubt about the wickedness of pirate crimes. Pirates were considered enemies to all humankind. As Neville Williams writes in Captains Outrageous, *public prosecutor Edmund Jennings put to public record what many authorities had said among themselves. At a trial in Virginia, Jennings thundered:*

"Piracy is the worst of crimes and pirates the worst of men. Nay, by these base actions they degrade themselves below the rank of men and become beasts of prey, and are worse than the worst of enemies, for they are governed by no laws of nations or of arms. They never give quarter or show mercy, but as they please themselves, live by rapine and violence, declare no war and yet are enemies of all mankind. They violate all the laws of God and man without any remorse or regret; they love mischief for mischief's sake, and will do what mischief they can, though it bring no advantage to themselves."

Once a pirate was caught by authorities, a trial was quickly held. Even if thirty or forty prisoners were involved, pirate trials lasted only a few days. Pirates had no lawyers or legal advice. They had to defend themselves, and most were seamen with little or no education. Most pirates could offer little in the way of defense other than "I was drunk the entire time." Many claimed they were forced into piracy against their will. This was difficult to prove. And authorities assembled the best legal minds to convict pirates. Judges and juries consisted of admirals, governors, solicitors general, secretaries of state, and other respected gentlemen.

A convicted pirate is prepared for his hanging on the execution docks at Wapping, England. Crowds often gathered to watch the gruesome executions and to hear the last words of the condemned.

The gallows was set up on the river's edge, near the low-tide mark. Once a pirate had died on the end of the hangman's rope, his body slowly bubbled beneath the sea as the tide rose. Tradition stated that three high tides must wash over the dead man before the body could be taken away. This was to stress the point that the crimes had been committed at sea.

If a pirate was well known, it was customary to display his corpse where it would be seen by all seamen entering and leaving port. This served as a warning to young men thinking of entering the pirate's trade.

One man was luckier than the rest. After William Duell was hanged in 1740, a surgeon washing his body for an autopsy noticed Duell was still breathing. Two hours later he was sitting up in a chair. Rather than hang him again, authorities sent Duell back to prison and eventually shipped him off to the colonies.

Hanging in Irons

Boston was a site of many pirate executions in the 1720s. And like Wapping, the dead bodies were often hung near the docks. In 1724, according to the *Boston Gazette*, John Rose, age twenty-seven, was "hung up in irons, to be a spectacle, and so a warning to others."[63] Later, William Fly was suspended from a gibbet at the entrance to the Charles River.

As a gruesome measure of preservation, corpses hung in chains were coated in tar. This preserved the body and discouraged

Captain Kidd's corpse hangs in chains, warning seafarers that piracy in not tolerated in that port.

flocks of crows and gulls that would otherwise eat it. After tarring, the body was laid into a harness of custom-made iron hoops and chains. It took a blacksmith quite some time to make the irons, and they were costly items. Although this grisly practice is well known, only a tiny percentage of pirates were gibbeted. Most were simply buried in anonymous paupers' graves.

Woodes Rogers Arrives in Nassau

Gruesome pirate punishment did little to stop piracy at its height in the early eighteenth century. With the likes of Blackbeard, Calico Jack, and other rogues based out of Nassau, the British government had to take serious action to flush the pirates permanently from the Bahamas. That action took the form of Woodes Rogers, who was born in Dorset, England, in 1679. Rogers was a former privateer and had sailed around the globe several times.

On July 24, 1718, Woodes Rogers arrived in Nassau harbor to an estimated two hundred ships docked in the harbor and more than one thousand pirates carousing onshore. Rogers brought with him a proclamation appointing him "Captain-General and Governor-in-Chief in and over Our Bahaman Islands." It was a long title but it meant one thing—the pirate days were over. Rogers also brought with him an Act of Grace, a royal pardon for all pirates who turned themselves in before September 5, 1718. The pardon demanded that pirates take an oath swearing they would stop piracy forever. After September 5, the buccaneers would be hunted down and hanged.

Before he even left his ship, Rogers was astonished to discover that, in negotiations with pirates, a majority said they were willing to accept the pardon. A few of the worst criminals, Blackbeard, Calico Jack, and Bartholomew Roberts among them, decamped for the high seas—they refused to quit the pirate life.

One pirate, Charles Vane, was not to leave so peacefully. As night fell on the ships of the Royal Navy, a series of explosions rocked the harbor and lit up the night. Vane had loaded a recently stolen French ship with explosives, cut it loose, and set it ablaze. The navy ships were forced to hurry out to sea to avoid the conflagration. In the morning, Vane ran up the pirate flag on his ship and sailed out to sea with a boatload of riches.

Pardoning the Pirates

On July 27, Rogers finally set foot on Bahamian soil. Upon landing, he was astounded to find two lines of drunken, filthy pirates, some three hundred in number. It was a ridiculous honor guard of ragged rogues firing volleys of musketry over their heads while shouting allegiance to England's King George. Rogers later recounted that he took the harbor's fort,

> where I read His Majesty's Commission in the presence of my officers, soldiers and about 300 of the people here, who re-

Despite the risk of execution, pirate Charles Vane refused to give up piracy.

ceived me under arms and readily surrendered, showing then many tokens of joy for the re-introductions of Government.[64]

When Rogers unrolled his fancy scrolls and shouted out words that appointed him master of all he saw, the bearded pirates gawked and laughed. As far as the eye could see, Nassau was dirty tents, wild pigs, overgrown trails, a few ramshackled huts, and stinking cesspools.

Rogers brought in his soldiers and started handing out pardons, eventually over six hundred in all. He offered each man a free plot of land on the condition he clear it and build a house within one year. He appointed the least criminal among them to government posts such as secretary general, chief justice, justices of the peace, marshals, and so on. From among the citizens, Rogers organized a militia and built a new eight-gun fort.

Punishing the Backsliders

After Rogers's initial success, events turned for the worse. It was a hot summer in New Providence and epidemics soon raged through the island. The ships that brought Rogers set out to sea lest all the navy men die of fever. As summer turned into autumn, many pirates drifted back to their old ways. A few former pirates who had become Rogers's most trusted agents went after these backsliders.

Former pirate captain Benjamin Hornigold was Rogers's chief pirate chaser. In October he captured a bunch of pirates who had accepted the pardon but continued at piracy. Rogers was to make an example of them. Of the ten men put to trial, only one was found not guilty. The others were condemned to death on December 12 at high noon. According to the Records Office, after "¾ of an hour spent by them in singing of psalms, the stage fell and they swung off."[65] After the executions, New Providence was no longer a safe haven for pirates.

Blackbeard's Nemesis

One alumnus of New Providence who never considered the king's pardon was the scoundrel known as Blackbeard. After leaving New Providence when Rogers arrived, Blackbeard and his crew terrorized the shipping lanes along the Atlantic coast. But Blackbeard had an ally in Charles Eden, who was the governor of North Carolina.

Most of the colonies had turned against piracy by 1717, but North Carolina was poor, with very little export trade. Eden granted Blackbeard and his crew an Act of Grace in return for a share of his loot. Blackbeard camped with his four hundred men and careened his four vessels openly on the Cape Fear and Pamlico Rivers. With the governor's approval, he openly sold his plundered booty on the streets of Bath.

But Blackbeard could not restrain his greed. In the spring of 1718 he blockaded the harbor of Charleston in the neighboring state of South Carolina. Blackbeard brazenly pillaged nine ships and held a member of the governor's council and his four-year-old son hostage. The pirate threatened to kill the man unless he received badly needed medical supplies.

Blackbeard's pirates soon overstayed their welcome in North Carolina. Their loutish behavior on the streets of Bath upset respectable merchants who wanted the pirates' trade, not

Blackbeard's and Vane's crews dance and party on the coast of North Carolina. Their brazen behavior soon made them unwelcome visitors in that state.

the pirates themselves. Before long the rascals began plundering any ship that came down Bath's rivers.

Governor Eden still took no action. But Alexander Spotswood, the governor of neighboring Virginia, decided to act. Spotswood detested pirates—especially Blackbeard—and the governor had the use of two men-of-war that were stationed as guard ships in the James River. In the fall of 1718 Spotswood heard that Blackbeard was planning to build a large base and fortress on North Carolina's Ocracoke Inlet. Spotswood decided to fight off the pirate, even though North Carolina was not in his jurisdiction.

The Governor, the Spy, and the Pirate

Governor Spotswood sent a secret agent to spy on Blackbeard. He wanted to know the pirate's personal habits and professional methods. The spy was also instructed to bring back a few coastal pilots who knew the inshore waters where Blackbeard was anchored. Spotswood held council with warship captains who said the Carolina sounds were too shallow for their men-of-war. The governor agreed to provide suitable vessels and the navy would provide the crew.

Spotswood posted a reward of £100 to any naval seaman who captured Blackbeard. Those who captured other pirate captains would receive £40. Lieutenants were worth £20, as were quartermasters, boatswains, and carpenters. An ordinary pirate brought a £10 reward. Spotswood planned in utmost secrecy, not even telling his council "for fear of Blackbeard's having intelligence, there being in this county an unaccountable inclination to favour pirates."[66]

Bringing Down the Brazen Blackbeard

On November 17, two shallow-draft naval sloops with sixty men set sail under the command of Lieutenant Robert Maynard. As day dawned on the 22nd, Maynard had Blackbeard's sloops in sight. Blackbeard was not surprised to see him. North Carolina's collector of customs, Tobias Knight, had heard of the operation and warned the pirate. Though the pirate had only eighteen men with him that morning, he was unfazed. Instead of preparing for battle, he spent his time drinking and carousing. Maynard prepared his troops. The next morning, they launched their attack.

Blackbeard's last stand soon became one of the greatest battles in pirate history. The pirate cursed at Maynard and swigged rum. Then he cut his cables and sailed away. One of the naval ships tried to blockade the pirate and was met by a vicious broadside that killed its commander and several men. The rigging was so badly damaged that this ship played no further role in the battle.

The wind died down, and Maynard, in the other ship, ordered his men to row over to Blackbeard's ship. A second broadside of partridge and small shot devastated Maynard's ship and wounded twenty-one of his crew. Maynard ordered all thirty-five of his men belowdecks.

Blackbeard launched another attack. He came alongside the naval sloop and threw aboard hand grenades full of small shot and scrap iron. Explosions and smoke engulfed the ship. Blackbeard ordered his pirates to jump on board and cut the enemy to pieces. He was the first across, lashing the two vessels together with a rope he carried.

Maynard ordered all men left standing to fight. The crews met head-on amid shouts

Blackbeard battles to the death with Captain Maynard. In the end, Maynard would emerge victorious.

and curses. Cutlasses clanged, pistols fired, and Maynard found himself face-to-face with the vicious Blackbeard. Both men grabbed pistols and fired at each other point-blank. It was at this moment, perhaps, that Blackbeard perceived the folly of drinking all night and all morning. With his unsteady hand, Blackbeard missed the naval officer. Maynard's shot, however, went straight into the pirate's body.

A Fight to the Death

Incredibly, Maynard's shot did nothing to stop Blackbeard. The bellowing pirate swung his cutlass and broke Maynard's sword in half. Maynard fell to the deck as Blackbeard drew back his cutlass to finish off the defenseless

lieutenant. At that moment, one of Maynard's men slashed Blackbeard across the throat. Maynard rolled away, but Blackbeard still fought on, screaming and swearing, blood spouting from his neck. Other navy men drew guns on Blackbeard and shot at him. Blackbeard grabbed another pistol, cocked it, then finally toppled over and fell to the deck.

With their leader dead, the other pirates surrendered. Ten, including Blackbeard, had been killed, nine were wounded. Maynard had ten dead and twenty-four wounded. Upon examining Blackbeard's dead body, Maynard found no less than twenty-five wounds—five from pistol shots. He ordered Blackbeard's head to be cut from his body. With this grisly trophy swinging from his bowsprit, Maynard sailed back to Virginia.

The death of Blackbeard marked the end of piracy in America's coastal waters. Governor Eden was never prosecuted for his dealings with Blackbeard and died three years later from yellow fever.

The Last—and Deadliest—Pirate

Today Bartholomew Roberts—Black Bart—is not as famous as his colleague Blackbeard. But in his day, Bart was the "Great Pyrate Roberts," undisputed king of the sea rovers. A Welshman with a dark complexion, Black Bart loved to dress in silk, velvet, and gold. Bart kept a tight rein on his crew, encouraging prayer, while forbidding gambling and drinking. In fact, Roberts was history's only known pirate who did not drink alcohol.

Blackbeard's ghastly head hangs from Maynard's bowsprit. Blackbeard's death foreshadowed the end of piracy in America.

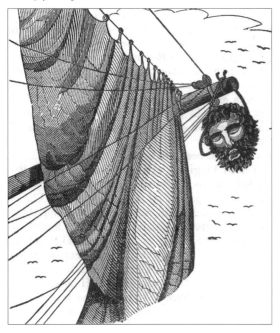

Though Black Bart preferred tea to rum, that did not make him any less feared. He crisscrossed the globe with a fleet of ships so large that naval squadrons turned away at mere sight of his flag, afraid to confront him. Even with a single ship, Black Bart performed amazing feats. With a ten-gun sloop and a crew of sixty, he took twenty-two ships lying at anchor in Newfoundland. With drums beating and trumpets blaring, the sixty pirates captured twelve hundred terror-stricken men. The pirates plundered and sank the entire fleet of merchantmen except for one brigantine that Bart used to carry the booty.

Roberts turned to piracy at the advanced age of thirty-six, not because he could not make a living any other way, but because he could not stand the snobbish manners of the upper-class merchants he knew. Captain Charles Johnson wrote that Roberts became a pirate "to get rid of the disagreeable Superiority of some Masters he was acquainted with . . . and [for] the Love of Novelty and Change."[67]

Black Bart was elected captain by his crew after his first pirate mission, when his ship's original captain was killed by Portuguese settlers on Princes Island. Bart leveled their town as revenge.

Heinous Acts at Sea

Roberts took his men to the Caribbean in 1720 and then north. He spent the summer plundering along the coast of New England and Newfoundland. He sailed to Africa and South America. By October 1720, the governor of the French Leewards in the Caribbean wrote that Bart had "seized, burned, or sunk 15 French and English vessels and one Dutch interloper of 42 guns at Dominica."[68]

Sailing right under the cannons on the island of St. Kitts, Roberts plundered and burned many vessels at anchor. Word got around that his crew was slicing off the ears of prisoners, using men for pistol practice, whipping them to death, and committing other heinous acts.

By the spring of 1721, there was little left for Roberts to steal, so he set off for Africa again. For another two seasons, the pirates plundered up and down the Guinea coast. On a single day Black Bart took eleven French, English, and Portuguese ships.

Roberts seemed invincible. But in February 1722, a fifty-gun Royal Navy warship, the *Swallow*, caught sight of the pirates near the Guinea coast. Captain Chaloner Ogle had been searching for Roberts for six months.

Roberts's Luck Runs Out

Roberts had been hiding along the African coast in snarled jungles, corkscrew rivers, and steamy swamps. When the pirate saw the *Swallow*, he thought it was a Portuguese merchant ship and sent one of his ships out to rob it. Ogle lured the pirates out to sea, killed ten, and took one hundred prisoner. Five days later, Ogle returned to where Roberts was at anchor.

The *Swallow* flew a French flag so Roberts would not be alarmed. The ruse did not work and Black Bart began sailing away while firing at Ogle's ship. The *Swallow* launched a broadside that toppled Roberts's mizzenmast. The pirates fired back. When the smoke

Giving Pirates a Break

English authorities kept trying to break the grip of pirates in the Caribbean. But people in New England gave pirates a break. By the late 1600s, Jamaica was no longer a safe haven for pirates, so many turned north, especially to Massachusetts, New York, and Rhode Island. In New York City respectable businessmen sold pirates gunpowder, food, and beer. Others set up clearinghouses for plunder. Authorities in Boston welcomed what they called "plate ships" from captains who insisted they had salvaged the gold and silver from sunken ships.

Pirates came to New England because they were freely pardoned there—even if they let it slip that they had not yet made their final voyages. The pardons cost quite a bit of money and were responsible for padding the bank accounts of quite a few governors. A royal proclamation against pirates was torn down by an angry Bostonian crowd. And almost overnight, North Carolina became a "pirate community without disguise," according to author Neville Williams.

In his book *Captains Outrageous*, Williams also describes the activities of Governor Benjamin Fletcher of New York who offered letters of protection to pirates. Fletcher made his fortune from nefarious dealings with sea scoundrels. He charged each pirate on a ship $100 to land in New York Harbor. Returning to New York from an incredibly successful looting in the Indian Ocean, pirate Thomas Tew

> was received and caressed by Governor Fletcher, dined and supped often with him and appeared with him publicly in his court. They also exchanged presents, such as gold watches.

The governor's wife and daughters were seen decked out in diamonds that had been meant for an Arabian princess. Fletcher's successor, Richard Coote, found New York a "thieves' kitchen," which he set in order.

cleared, they saw Roberts's body slumped on the deck, his throat ripped open by a blast of grapeshot. Black Bart's corpse—in all its fine gold and silk—was heaved over the side by his sobbing men. Bartholomew Roberts had captured more than four hundred ships in four years.

The death of Roberts unnerved his crew. Without his skill, bravery, and cunning, they were confused and lost. By early afternoon, Bart's crew could fight no more. The grizzled pirates began drinking heavily. Some were too drunk to stand by the time they surrendered to Ogle.

Ogle's operations rounded up 264 men. Of these, 77 were black Africans and 187 were white men. Several were seamen and passengers recently captured by Bart during his raids along the African coast. The pirates were shackled together and thrown into a vast, dark cavern under the Cape Coast Castle—England's main fort in Africa.

On March 28, 169 men faced the largest pirate trial ever held in Cape Coast Castle's Great Hall. Nineteen men had died of their wounds before the trial began. Seventy-four men, including musicians, were acquitted. Fifty-two were sentenced to death and hanged within three weeks.

At the conclusion of the trial, the president of the court read the verdict.

> Ye and each of you are adjudged and sentenced to be carried back to the place from whence you came, from thence to the place of execution outside the gates of this castle, and there within the flood marks to be hanged by the neck, till you are dead, dead, dead. And the Lord have mercy upon your souls. After this, ye and each of you shall be taken down and your bodies hung in chains.[69]

In April 1722, fifty-two pirates were hanged "like dogs" in batches over a two-week period. Seventeen pirates were sent off to prison in London, but thirteen of those men died of fever on the way back to England. Twenty pirates were sentenced to seven years hard labor in the gold mines of Africa. None outlived his sentence.

The Close of the Golden Age

With the mass hangings on the African coast, the golden age of piracy drew to a close. The bodies of eighteen men were coated in tar and strung from gibbets on the hills overlooking the harbor. The rotting corpses drifting in the wind gave notice that there was no place left for pirates in a world dominated by merchants, kings, and navies.

The men of Black Bart's crew represented only a small portion of active pirates. But after his death the rest of the world's freebooters virtually disappeared. Gold and riches continued to crisscross the oceans, but cargoes were better guarded than ever before. As trade increased, nations could afford bigger and more efficient navies. It became more lucrative for governors and officials to be honest. It was the Age of Enlightenment in Europe, and there was a general greater sense of responsibility by nations toward a civilized standard of behavior. In face of this, the pirates of the golden age simply evaporated like wispy fog in the hot morning sun.

Then and Now: Pirates into the Twentieth Century

The curtain fell on piracy's golden age in the 1720s. But it rose again fifty-five years later when American revolutionaries fought England for their freedom. The Revolutionary War was fought at sea by sailors and privateers. The tiny American navy had only thirty-four ships. But more than four hundred privateers attacked British merchants, crippling trade. As in centuries before, those who lost ships to privateers called them pirates. But to Americans fighting for their rights, the privateers were heroes. When the United States later fought England in the War of 1812, naval privateers once again lashed out at British shipping.

By the mid-1800s, technology helped put an end to piracy. The navies of Britain and the United States had steam-powered ships that

American and British ships broadside each other during the Revolutionary War. The privateers who fought for America's independence during the war were revered as heroes, not as pirates.

could sail anywhere, even on windless days. Pirates could not afford expensive steam ships and were helpless before their power. By 1850, only a handful of pirates were left on the seven seas.

Modern Pirates

With the availability of high-tech weapons and cheap, powerful boats, piracy has experienced a comeback in modern times. Pirates prowl the waters along the coast of Brazil, the west coast of Africa, and in the Far East, especially in the Strait of Malacca. In 1992 there were more than ninety attacks on shipping in the waters between Sumatra and Singapore. Many of the pirates in that area operate in the channels between the islands of Indonesia.

With powerful fishing boats, they attack under the cover of darkness. Once alongside their prey, today's pirates climb aboard with grappling hooks. As in the old days, the small crews of merchant ships have little defense against the armed, determined pirates. Modern pirates work quickly, cleaning out a boat in ten or twenty minutes.

Acts of piracy have flared up since those days in the 1720s, but none have captured the public imagination like those "scurvy dogs" of the golden age. For all their dastardly deeds, the pirates touched something deep in the soul of the common people: the fantasy of breaking society's rules, the lure of the sea, and the dream of untold riches. For all their cruel tortures, desperation, and hangings, the long shadows and mythical deeds of the buccaneers still call from across the centuries.

Notes

Introduction: The Famous Age of Pirates

1. Quoted in Douglas Botting, *The Pirates*. Alexandria, VA: Time-Life Books, 1978, p. 6.
2. Quoted in David Cordingly, *Under the Black Flag*. New York: Random House, 1995, p. 6.

Chapter 1: The Great Age of Piracy

3. Quoted in David Cordingly and John Falconer, *Pirates Fact and Fiction*. New York: Cross River Press, 1992.
4. Bernal Díaz del Castillo, *The Conquest of New Spain*. New York: Penguin Books, 1963, p. 216.
5. Quoted in Richard Platt, *Pirate*. New York: Knopf, 1994, p. 18.
6. Francis Drake, *The World Encompassed*. 1628. Reprint: New York: Da Capo Press, 1969, pp. 59–60.
7. Quoted in Jenifer G. Marx, in *Pirates: Terror on the High Seas from the Caribbean to the South China Sea*. Ed. David Cordingly. Atlanta: Turner Publishing, 1996, p. 37.
8. Quoted in Cordingly, *Under the Black Flag*, p. 202.
9. Quoted in Cordingly, *Under the Black Flag*, p. 202.
10. Quoted in Marcus Rediker, *Between the Devil and the Deep Blue Sea*. Cambridge, England: Cambridge University Press, 1987, p. 258.
11. Quoted in Rediker, *Between the Devil and the Deep Blue Sea*, p. 260.
12. Quoted in Cordingly, *Under the Black Flag*, p. 16.
13. Quoted in Cordingly, *Under the Black Flag*, p. 18.
14. Quoted in Cordingly, *Under the Black Flag*, p. 18.
15. Quoted in Neville Williams, *Captains Outrageous*. New York: Macmillan, 1962, p. 59.
16. Quoted in Botting, *The Pirates*, p. 31.

Chapter 2: The Captain and Crew

17. Quoted in Rediker, *Between the Devil and the Deep Blue Sea*, p. 260.
18. Quoted in Rediker, *Between the Devil and the Deep Blue Sea*, p. 262.
19. John Esquemeling, *The Buccaneers of America*. Glorieta, NM: Rio Grande Press, 1992, p. 60.
20. Esquemeling, *The Buccaneers of America*, p. 60.
21. Quoted in Rediker, *Between the Devil and the Deep Blue Sea*, p. 262.
22. Quoted in Richard Platt, *Pirate*, p. 48.
23. Quoted in Cordingly and Falconer, *Pirates Fact and Fiction*.
24. Quoted in Marx, in *Pirates*, ed. David Cordingly, p. 101.
25. Quoted in Cordingly, *Under the Black Flag*, p. 61.
26. Quoted in Cordingly, *Under the Black Flag*, p. 61.
27. Quoted in Botting, *The Pirates*, p. 150.
28. Quoted in Botting, *The Pirates*, p. 151.
29. Quoted in Botting, *The Pirates*, p. 151.

Chapter 3: Sailing over the Bounty Main

30. Quoted in Cordingly, *Under the Black Flag*, p. 159.
31. Quoted in Platt, *Pirate*, p. 24.

32. Quoted in Botting, *The Pirates*, p. 44.
33. Quoted in Cordingly, *Under the Black Flag*, p. 93.
34. Quoted in Peter Newark, *The Crimson Book of Pirates*. London: Jupiter Books, 1978, p. 29.
35. Esquemeling, *The Buccaneers of America*, p. 297.
36. Quoted in Platt, *Pirate*, p. 42.
37. Esquemeling, *The Buccaneers of America*, pp. 394–95.
38. Quoted in Cordingly, *Under the Black Flag*, p. 94.

Chapter 4: Into Action on the High Seas

39. Quoted in Botting, *The Pirates*, p. 57.
40. Quoted in Cordingly, *Under the Black Flag*, p. 106.
41. Quoted in Cordingly, *Under the Black Flag*, p. 123.
42. Quoted in Botting, *The Pirates*, p. 60.
43. Esquemeling, *The Buccaneers of America*.
44. Newark, *The Crimson Book of Pirates*, p. 33.
45. Quoted in Cordingly, *Under the Black Flag*, p. 108.
46. Quoted in Cordingly, *Under the Black Flag*, p. 108.
47. Quoted in Platt, *Pirate*, p. 52.
48. Quoted in Cordingly and Falconer, *Pirates Fact and Fiction*.
49. Quoted in Botting, *The Pirates*, p. 127.

Chapter 5: Exotic Ports of Call

50. Esquemeling, *The Buccaneers of America*, p. 75.
51. Quoted in Marx, in *Pirates*, ed. David Cordingly, p. 40.
52. Esquemeling, *The Buccaneers of America*, p. 73.
53. Esquemeling, *The Buccaneers of America*, pp. 102–103.
54. Quoted in Marx, in *Pirates*, ed. David Cordingly, p. 50.
55. Quoted in Marx, in *Pirates*, ed. David Cordingly, p. 50.
56. Quoted in Marx, in *Pirates*, ed. David Cordingly, p. 50.
57. Quoted in Cordingly, *Under the Black Flag*, p. 141.
58. Quoted in Cordingly, *Under the Black Flag*, p. 46.
59. Quoted in Cordingly, *Under the Black Flag*, p. 52.
60. Quoted in Marx, in *Pirates*, ed. David Cordingly, p. 54.
61. Quoted in Botting, *The Pirates*, p. 140.

Chapter 6: The Hunters Become the Hunted

62. Quoted in Cordingly, *Under the Black Flag*, p. 202.
63. Quoted in Cordingly, *Under the Black Flag*, p. 204.
64. Quoted in Cordingly, *Under the Black Flag*, pp. 152–53.
65. Quoted in Cordingly, *Under the Black Flag*, p. 154.
66. Quoted in Botting, *The Pirates*, p. 149.
67. Quoted in Marx, in *Pirates*, ed. David Cordingly, p. 119.
68. Quoted in Marx, in *Pirates*, ed. David Cordingly, p. 121.
69. Quoted in Cordingly, *Under the Black Flag*, p. 233.

Glossary

boatswain, or bosun: A ship's officer in charge of sails, rigging, and anchors.

bow: The front of a ship.

bowsprit: A stout wooden pole extending forward from the front of a ship.

brig: A ship with two square-rigged masts and sails on the lower part of the mainmast.

brigantine: A two-masted vessel with a square-rigged foremast and a mainmast with fore-and-aft square sails.

broadside: The firing of all guns on one side of a ship at the same time.

buccaneer: Originally the term applied to hunters of wild pigs on the island of Hispaniola. Later used to describe the pirates and privateers who plundered ships and towns in the West Indies, South America, and Central America in the late 1600s.

careen: To roll a ship over on its side and clean the seaweed and barnacles from its bottom.

colors: Flags flown by a vessel.

flagship: A ship commanded by an admiral and flying the admiral's flag.

fore: The front part of a ship.

galleon: A large Spanish sailing vessel of the fifteenth and sixteenth centuries.

helm: The tiller or wheel that controls the rudder, or steering mechanism, of a ship.

letter of marque: A license issued by a king, queen, or member of government that gave a ship's captain the right to plunder an enemy's ships. Pirates with letters of marque were called privateers.

mast: A heavy pole that rises above a ship's deck and holds the sails.

mizzenmast: The middle mast of a three-masted ship.

privateer: A vessel or the commander and crew of a vessel with a letter of marque authorizing the men aboard to plunder an enemy's ship.

schooner: A two-masted vessel with fore-and-aft sails rigged on both masts.

sloop: A vessel having one fore-and-aft rigged mast with a mainsail and a single front or foresail.

spar: A stout wooden pole used for the mast or bowsprit of a ship.

swivel gun: A small gun or cannon mounted on a swivel so it could be turned to fire.

waggoner: A sea atlas or volume of sea maps and charts.

For Further Reading

Douglas Botting, *The Pirates*. Alexandria, VA: Time-Life Books, 1978. A big, fun, colorful book with pirate paintings, informational sidebars, woodcuttings, maps, and exciting, well-written text. There are many renderings of ships with cross sections showing interiors and workings.

James Burney, *History of the Buccaneers of America*. London: George Allen and Unwin, 1951. First published in 1816, this book is another original source of much of today's pirate material.

David Cordingly, *Under the Black Flag*. New York: Random House, 1995. David Cordingly, an Oxford graduate, is the modern pirate expert who set up a museum exhibit entitled "Pirates Fact and Fiction." It opened in England in 1992 and went on to become one of the most popular exhibits ever mounted by the National Maritime Museum in Sussex. This book goes into great detail and has a wealth of information on pirate topics.

David Cordingly, ed., *Pirates: Terror on the High Seas from the Caribbean to the South China Sea*. Atlanta: Turner Publishing, 1996. Another big, colorful book, this one edited by pirate expert David Cordingly. Covers pirate activities in detail from the buccaneers to the American Revolution to the South China Sea.

David Cordingly and John Falconer, *Pirates Fact and Fiction*. New York: Cross River Press, 1992. Another great book by pirate expert David Cordingly. This is an easy-to-read book with a lot of interesting facts.

Daniel Defoe, *The Life and Strange Surprising Adventures of Robinson Crusoe, of York, Mariner*. New York: Signet Books, 1996. Defoe's book is not about pirates but about a young man who has many adventures at sea, including being shipwrecked and washed up on a deserted island. The work is said to be the first English novel.

John Esquemeling, *The Buccaneers of America*. Glorieta, NM: Rio Grande Press, 1992. Esquemeling's book, first published in 1642, was a best-seller for centuries. Esquemeling was originally a slave who became a buccaneer and traveled with Henry Morgan during the sack of Panama. Besides dozens of eyewitness descriptions of pirate activity, Esquemeling goes into great detail describing the plants, animals, and people who populated the Caribbean in the seventeenth century. This book provided a wealth of information for all other pirate books that were to follow. The old-fashioned text and sentence structure is a little tough to read but worth the trouble.

Stuart Kallen, *Ghosts of the Seven Seas*. Minneapolis: Abdo & Daughters, 1991. A children's book that details various folklore, superstitions, and ghost stories associated with the sea.

Richard Platt, *Pirate*. New York: Knopf, 1994. One of the great Eyewitness Books with excellent pictures that show many items a pirate saw during his career at sea.

Jane Shuter, *Exquemelin and Pirates of the Caribbean*. Austin, TX: Raintree Steck-Vaughn, 1995. A young-adult book with many quotes from Exquemelin (Esquemeling) and a general explanation of the pirate's life and times in easy-to-read language.

Edward Rowe Snow, *True Tales of Buried Treasure*. New York: Dodd, Mead & Company, 1951. An older but popular book about buried treasures found on sunken ships and ashore. Author reveals the sites of sixty recovered treasures and hints at locations where more may be found. Most, but not all, of the treasures were once pirate loot.

Robert Louis Stevenson, *Treasure Island*. New York: Charles Scribner & Sons, 1981. Originally published in 1911, Robert Louis Stevenson's book is *the* pirate classic, and the source for most images people have of pirates. A beautifully written book about buried treasure, desert islands, and Long John Silver, *Treasure Island* is a must-read for anyone interested in pirates.

Dennis Wepman, *Hernán Cortés*. New York: Chelsea House Publishers, 1986. A children's book detailing the actions of Hernán Cortés and the events that climaxed in his total destruction of the Aztec Empire. A very good reference with many insights into the great power struggle that was the beginning of Spanish rule in the West.

Websites

Beej's Pirate Image Archive
http://www.ecst.csuchico.edu/~beej/pirates/
Pictures of famous (and not-so-famous) pirates, including Francis L'Olonnais, Blackbeard, and Anne Bonny. Also has pictures of battles, maps, pirate tortures, and pirate fun.

Blackbeard
http://ocracoke-nc.com/blackbeard/
Everything you have always wanted to know about Blackbeard, including his twenty-seven-month reign, his blockade of Charleston, his women, vivid details of his death, and where to see his skull on display. One of several websites dedicated to Blackbeard.

No Quarter Given
http://www.discover.net/~nqgiven/index.html
This is a great on-line pirate magazine with up-to-the-minute information about pirates, including movie guides, upcoming pirate events, and book reviews. Anyone who loves pirates can spend hours with No Quarter Given.

Pirate's Home Page
http://orion.it.luc.edu/~tgibson/pirates/pirates.html
This site has much general information about pirates and links to other piratical sites.

Yahoo's Link to Pirates Pages
http://www.yahoo.com/Arts/Humanities/History/Maritime_History/Pirates/
This page has links to many great pirate web pages, including Pirate's Week, which highlights pirate events that took place during this week in history. Also included are links to several Blackbeard pages, commercial deep-sea salvage operations, pirate dictionaries and rope-tying guides, *National Geographic* pirate articles, and other pirate pages.

Works Consulted

Bernal Díaz del Castillo, *The Conquest of New Spain*. New York: Penguin Books, 1963. A fascinating book that details the first European encounters with the Aztecs.

Francis Drake, *The World Encompassed*. 1628. Reprint: New York: Da Capo Press, 1969. A reissue of the original book written by Sir Francis Drake that records his privateering and global circumnavigation. Written in old-style English, the book is somewhat difficult to read, but Drake's straight-ahead style, dry wit, and descriptions of plundering the biggest treasure ever stolen make this book a valuable first-person resource.

Peter Earle, *The Sack of Panama*. New York: Viking Press, 1981. A definitive and fascinating account of Henry Morgan's sack of Panama in 1671. Extremely well researched.

William Jay Jacobs, *Pizarro: Conqueror of Peru*. New York: Franklin Watts, 1994. A children's book about Francisco Pizarro, the Spaniard who conquered the Incas.

J. Franklin Jameson, *Privateering and Piracy in the Colonial Period*. New York: Augustus M. Kelly, 1970. Originally edited in 1923, this book is a compendium of eighteenth-century ships' logs, court records, depositions, letters, and official documents that detail the minutiae of government correspondence, pirates' plunder, and pirate trials.

Albert Marrin, *The Sea Rovers*. New York: Atheneum, 1984. A source of information about pirates and privateers written in a swashbuckling language and illustrated with old prints, engravings, maps, and diagrams.

Peter Newark, *The Crimson Book of Pirates*. London: Jupiter Books, 1978. This book is an enthralling excursion into the life and times of pirate captains such as Blackbeard and Francis L'Olonnais.

William Pratt, *Journals of Two Cruises Aboard the American Privateer Yankee*. New York: Macmillan, 1967. Originally written in 1812, this book gives a fascinating—but sometimes dryly worded—description of life aboard a privateer during the War of 1812.

Marcus Rediker, *Between the Devil and the Deep Blue Sea*. Cambridge, England: Cambridge University Press, 1987. A scholarly work about men of the sea. Rediker dissects the social and economic conditions of sailors from 1700 to 1750. Full of facts and figures, the book gives the details of a merchantman's life, including pay scale, language, culture, violence, discipline, and so on. The last chapter is about pirates and, from the previous chapters, we can see what drove honest sailors into a life of piracy.

Robert C. Ritchie, *Captain Kidd and the War Against the Pirates*. Cambridge, MA: Harvard University Press, 1986. A detailed account of the life and times of Captain Kidd. Helps the reader understand why a man who started out as a well-to-do privateer ended up swinging in the wind, hanged as a low-life pirate. Features pirates, politics, power, and buried treasure.

Alfred Sternbeck, *Filibusters and Buccaneers*. New York: Books for Libraries Press, 1972. A reprint of a book originally published in 1942 that gives insight into the life of famous privateers and pirates such as Drake, Roberts, and others.

C. Keith Wilbur, *Pirates and Patriots of the Revolution*. Old Saybrook, CT: Globe Pequot Press, 1984. A vividly illustrated book about life aboard a privateer ship during the American Revolution. There are descriptions, drawings, and diagrams showing sail riggings, hull construction, ships' cannons, personal arms, battle tactics, sea chanteys, and other real-life details of eighteenth-century sailors' lives.

Neville Williams, *Captains Outrageous*. New York: Macmillan, 1962. A book that focuses on the deeds and actions of pirate captains. The book is written in chronological order from the 1200s to the mid-1800s.

A. B. C. Wipple, *Pirate: Rascals of the Caribbean*. New York: Doubleday, 1957. A swashbuckling history of pirates who inhabited the Spanish Main.

Index

storms, 46
Strait of Malacca, 83
Sumatra, 83
superstitions, 46
surgeons, 25
Swallow, 80
swords, 49, 50
syphilis, 43

Teach, Edward. *See* Black-
  beard
telescopes, 39
Tenochtitlán, 13
Tew, Thomas, 80
Thomas, Dorthy, 33

Tortuga, 25, 60, 61, 62
tortures, 53–55, 61–62, 80
treasure, buried, 57
Treasure Island, 10
treasure ships, 13, 18
trials, 72
typhoid, 42
typhus, 42, 43

Under the Black Flag (Cordingly), 65
United States, 82
useless islands, 18–19

Vane, Charles, 49, 74–75

vermin, 42, 44

waggoners, 39
walking the plank, 27
Wapping, England, 71–72
Whydah, 56–57
Wickstead, John, 50
Wilbur, C. Keith, 52
Williams, Neville, 72
  on Fletcher, 80
Windward Passage, 61
women pirates, 31–34

yellow fever, 42
Young Folks magazine, 10

Picture Credits

About the Author

Stuart A. Kallen is the author of more than one hundred nonfiction books for children and young adults. He has written on subjects ranging from dinosaurs to Soviet history to Einstein's theory of relativity. His fascination with pirates began as a little boy while vacationing on Cape Cod. Mr. Kallen lives in San Diego, California, where he hopes to find sunken treasure some day.